GRIMMY™

Inc.

Grimmy's Flea Circus

by Mike Peters

TOR®

A TOM DOHERTY ASSOCIATES BOOK
NEW YORK

This is a work of fiction. All the characters and events portrayed in this book are either products of the author's imagination or are used fictitiously.

GRIMMY™: GRIMMY'S FLEA CIRCUS

www.grimmy.com

This book contains material previously published in a trade edition as *Grimmy: The Revenge of Grimmzilla.*

A Tor Book
Published by Tom Doherty Associates, LLC
175 Fifth Avenue
New York, NY 10010

www.tor.com

Tor® is a registered trademark of Tom Doherty Associates, LLC.

ISBN: 0-812-54921-X

First edition: July 2000
First mass market edition: June 2001

Printed in the United States of America

0   9   8   7   6   5   4   3   2   1

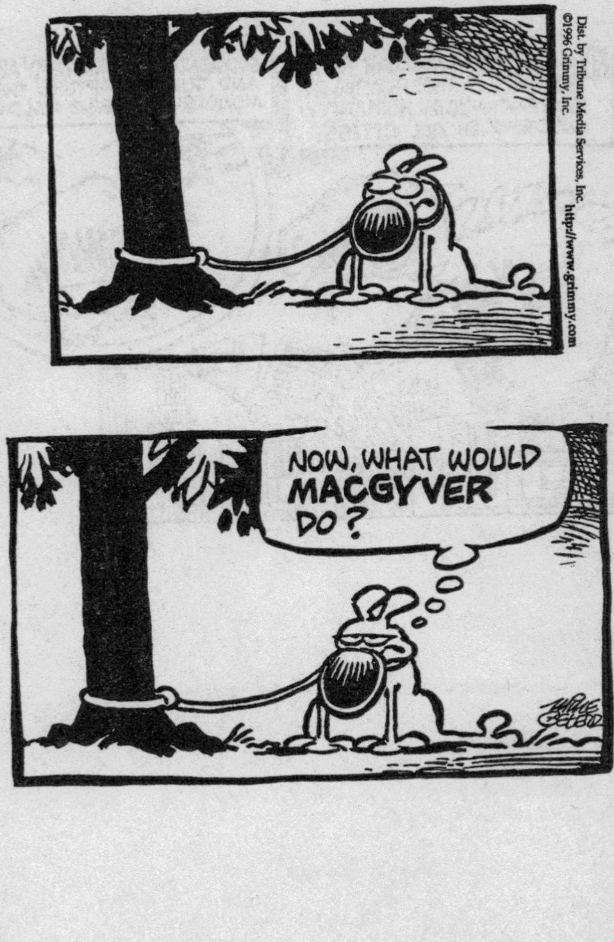
NOW, WHAT WOULD **MACGYVER** DO?

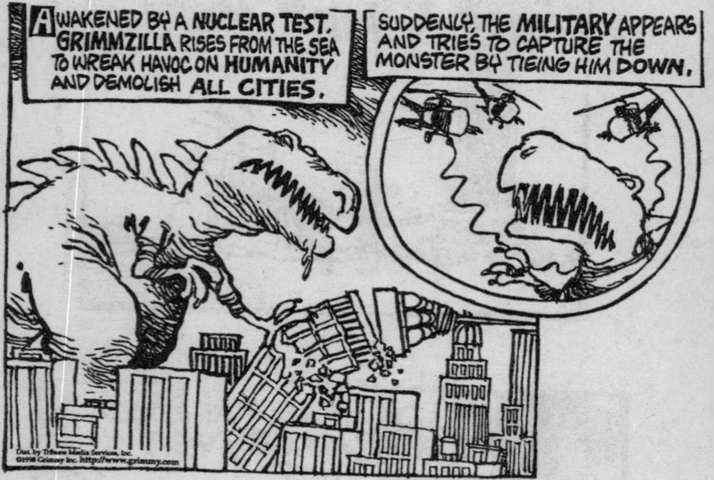
AWAKENED BY A NUCLEAR TEST, GRIMMZILLA RISES FROM THE SEA TO WREAK HAVOC ON HUMANITY AND DEMOLISH ALL CITIES.
SUDDENLY, THE MILITARY APPEARS AND TRIES TO CAPTURE THE MONSTER BY TIEING HIM DOWN.
Dist. by Tribune Media Services, Inc.
©1998 Grimmy Inc. http://www.grimmy.com

BUT GRIMMZILLA IS TOO STRONG FOR THEIR PITIFUL RESTRAINTS AND DRAGS HIS CAPTORS WITH HIM...
GRIMM, CAN'T YOU JUST GO FOR WALKS LIKE OTHER DOGS?

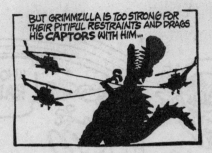

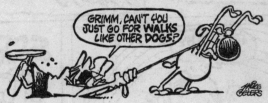

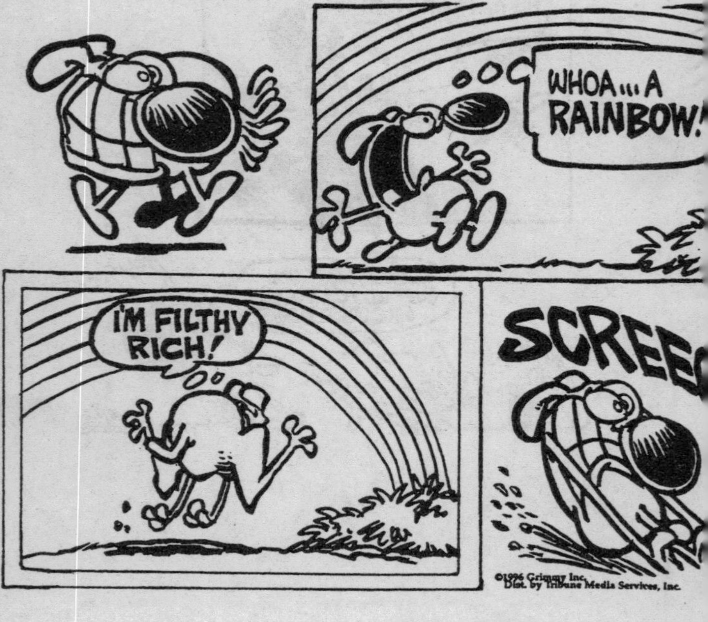
WHOA... A RAINBOW!
I'M FILTHY RICH!
SCREE
©1996 Grimmy Inc.
Dist. by Tribune Media Services, Inc.

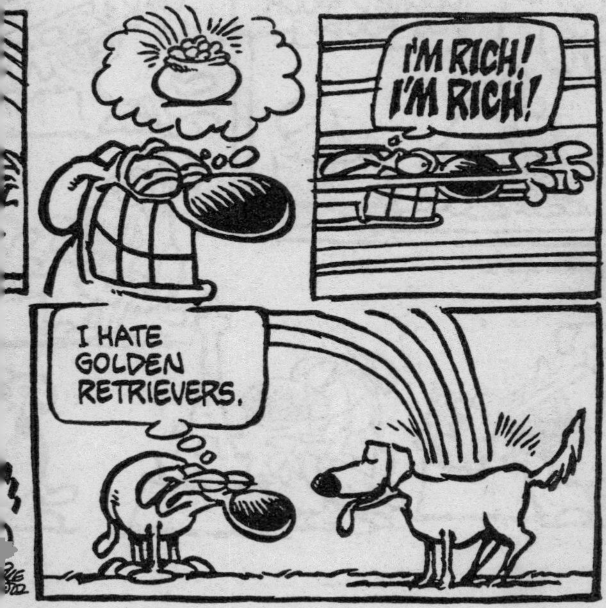
I'M RICH! I'M RICH!
I HATE GOLDEN RETRIEVERS.

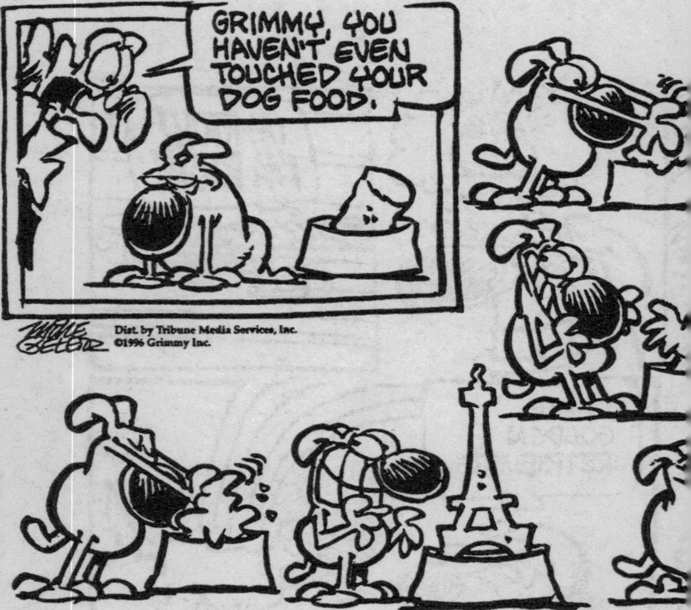
GRIMMY, YOU HAVEN'T EVEN TOUCHED YOUR DOG FOOD.

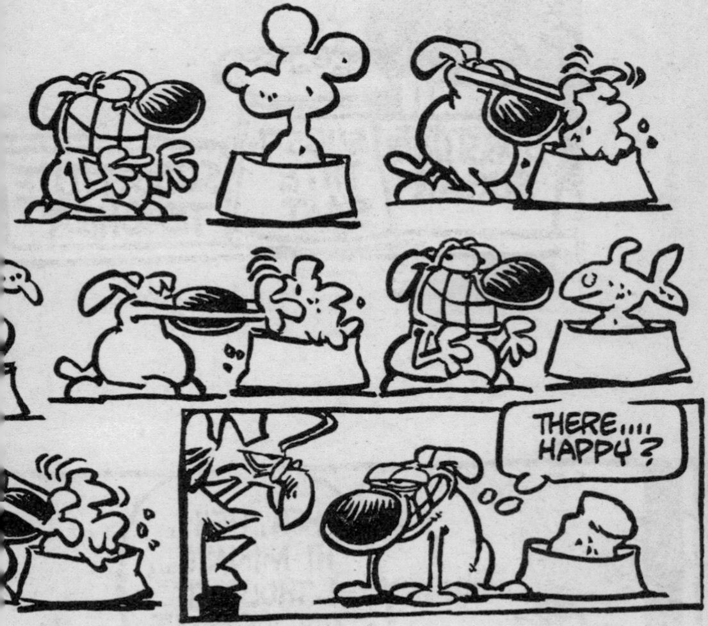
THERE.... HAPPY?

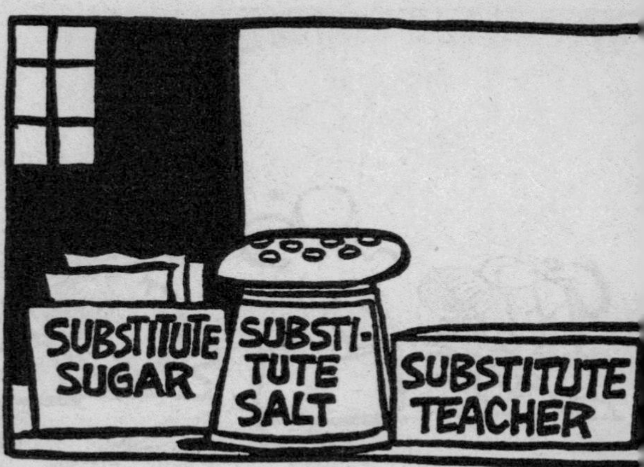
SUBSTITUTE SUGAR
SUBSTI-TUTE SALT
SUBSTITUTE TEACHER

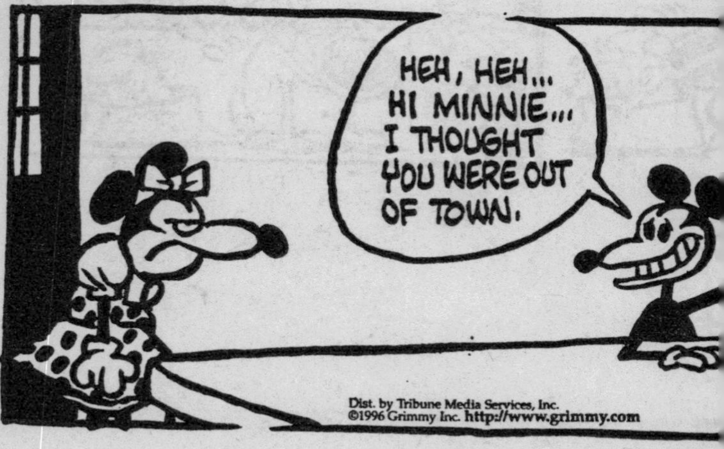
HEH, HEH... HI MINNIE... I THOUGHT YOU WERE OUT OF TOWN.
Dist. by Tribune Media Services, Inc.
©1996 Grimmy Inc. http://www.grimmy.com

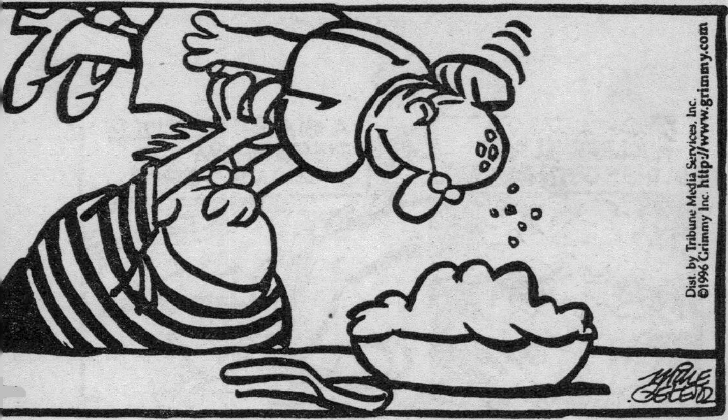
Dist. by Tribune Media Services, Inc.
©1996 Grimmy Inc. http://www.grimmy.com

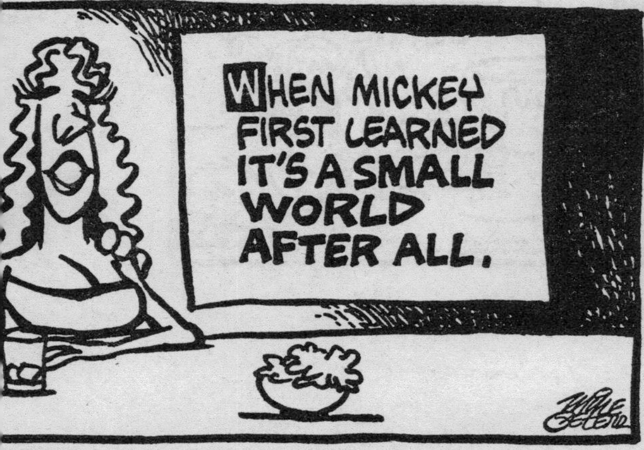
WHEN MICKEY FIRST LEARNED IT'S A SMALL WORLD AFTER ALL.

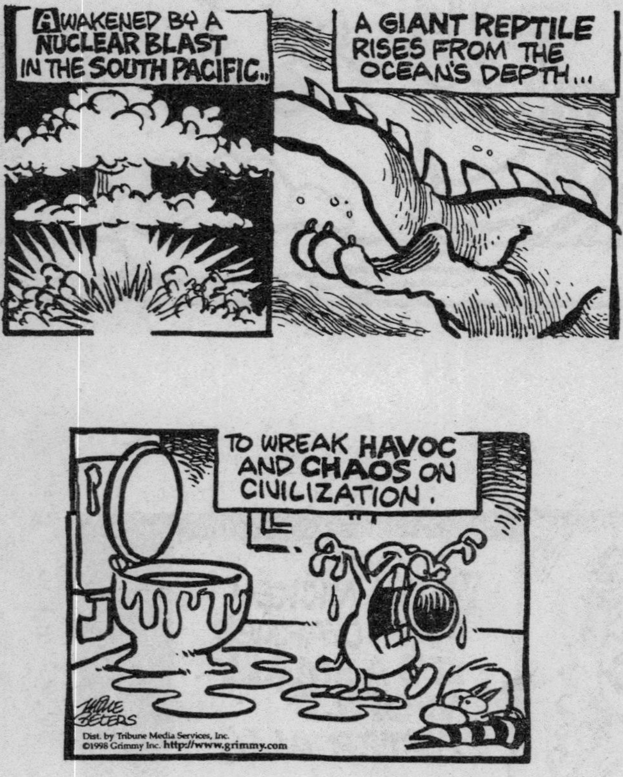
AWAKENED BY A NUCLEAR BLAST IN THE SOUTH PACIFIC..
A GIANT REPTILE RISES FROM THE OCEAN'S DEPTH...
TO WREAK HAVOC AND CHAOS ON CIVILIZATION.
MIKE PETERS
Dist. by Tribune Media Services, Inc.
©1998 Grimmy Inc. http://www.grimmy.com

GRIMMZILLA DEMOLISHES THE CITY WHILE HELICOPTERS HOVER OVERHEAD...
SUDDENLY HE JUMPS UP AND GRABS THE COPTER BLADES.
Dist. by Tribune Media Services, Inc. ©1998 Grimmy Inc. http://www.grimmy.com
MIKE PETERS
GRIMM, GET OFF THE CEILING FAN!

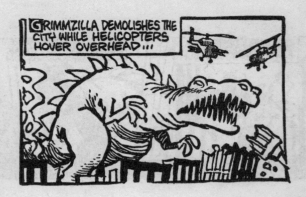

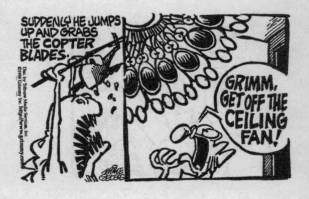

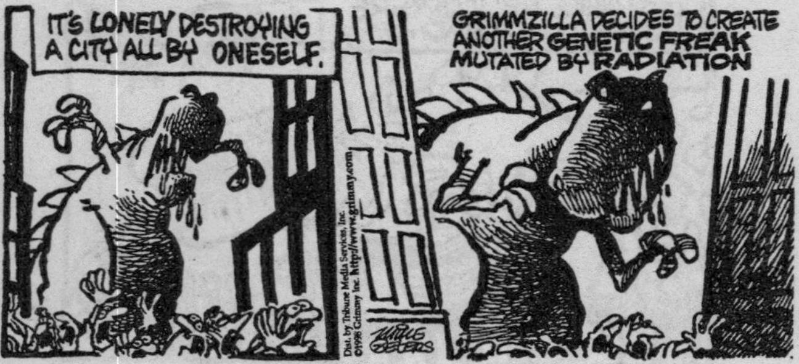
IT'S LONELY DESTROYING A CITY ALL BY ONESELF.
GRIMMZILLA DECIDES TO CREATE ANOTHER GENETIC FREAK MUTATED BY RADIATION
Dist. by Tribune Media Services, Inc.
©1998 Grimmy Inc. http://www.grimmy.com

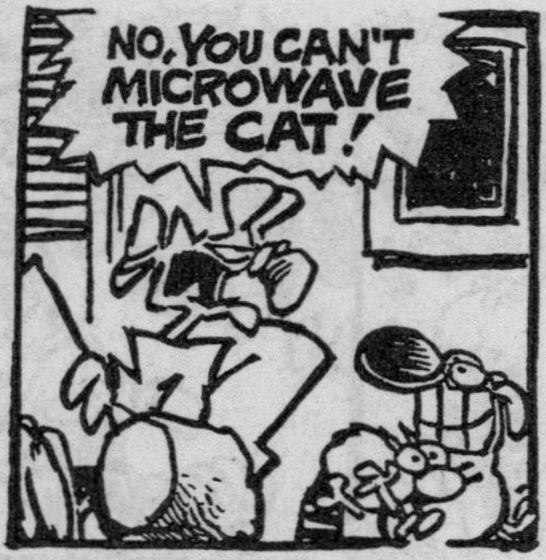
NO, YOU CAN'T MICROWAVE THE CAT!

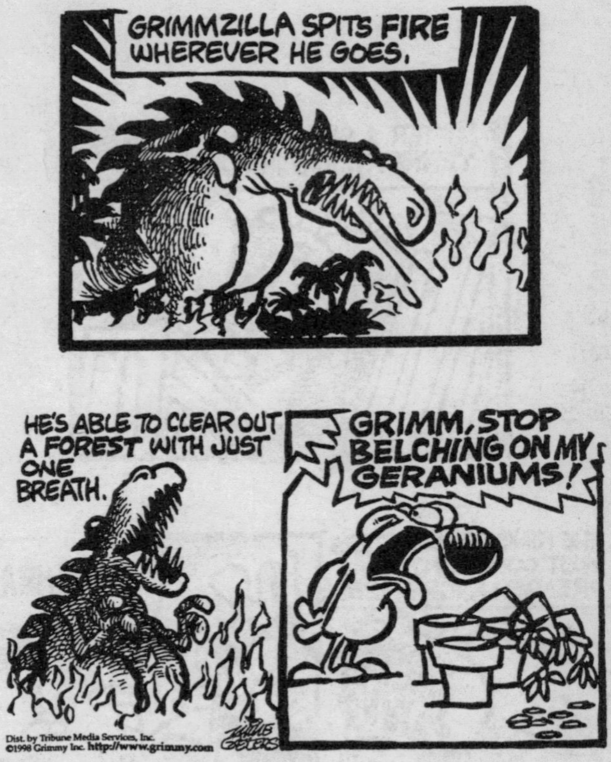
GRIMMZILLA SPITS FIRE WHEREVER HE GOES.
HE'S ABLE TO CLEAR OUT A FOREST WITH JUST ONE BREATH.
GRIMM, STOP BELCHING ON MY GERANIUMS!
Dist. by Tribune Media Services, Inc.
©1998 Grimmy Inc. http://www.grimmy.com
MIKE PETERS

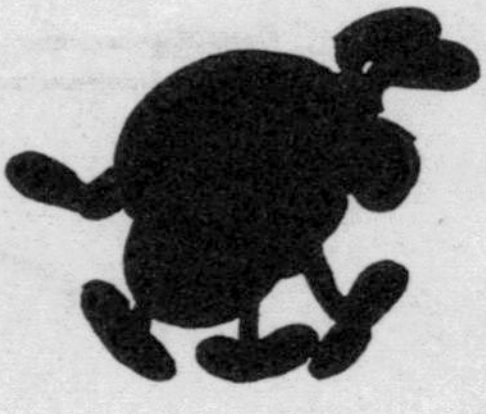

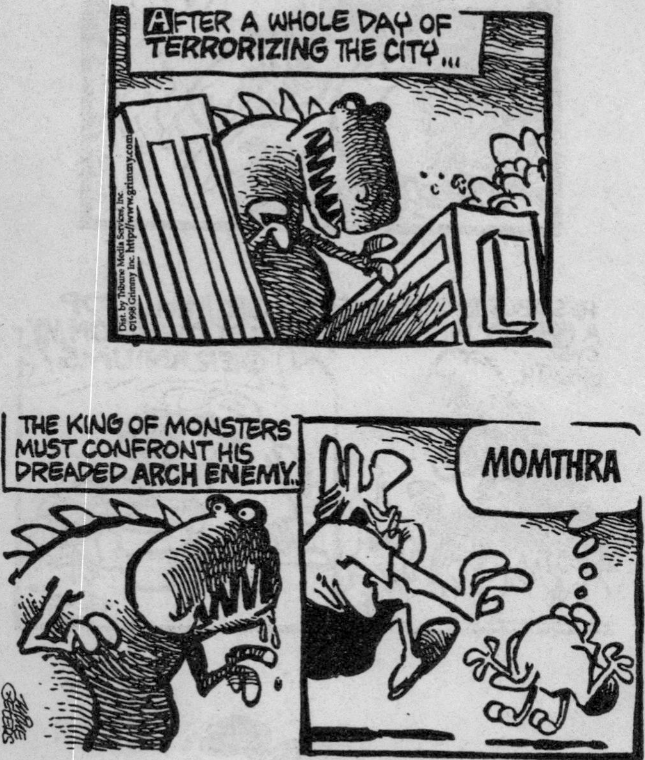
AFTER A WHOLE DAY OF TERRORIZING THE CITY...
Dist. by Tribune Media Services, Inc. ©1998 Grimmy Inc. http://www.grimmy.com
THE KING OF MONSTERS MUST CONFRONT HIS DREADED ARCH ENEMY...
MOMTHRA

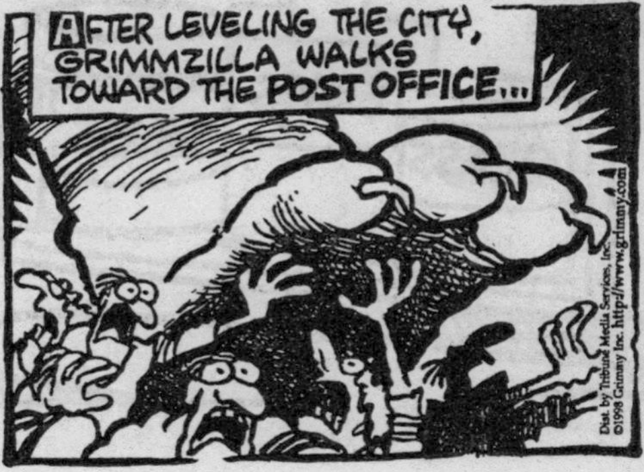
AFTER LEVELING THE CITY, GRIMMZILLA WALKS TOWARD THE POST OFFICE...
Dist. by Tribune Media Services, Inc.
©1998 Grimmy Inc. http://www.grimmy.com

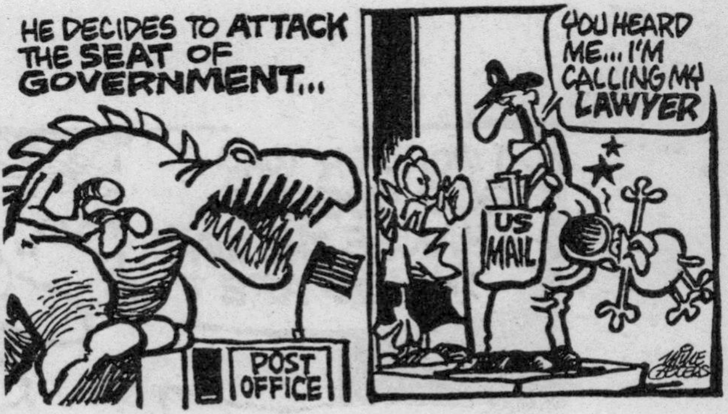
HE DECIDES TO ATTACK THE SEAT OF GOVERNMENT...
POST OFFICE
YOU HEARD ME... I'M CALLING MY LAWYER
US MAIL

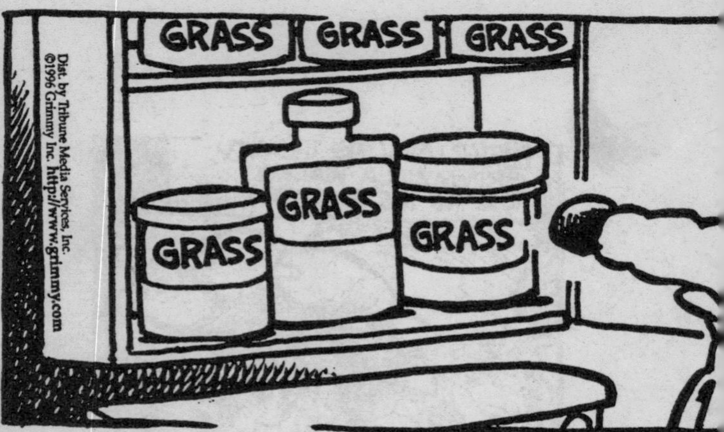
Dist. by Tribune Media Services, Inc.
©1996 Grimmy Inc. http://www.grimmy.com
GRASS GRASS GRASS
GRASS
GRASS
GRASS

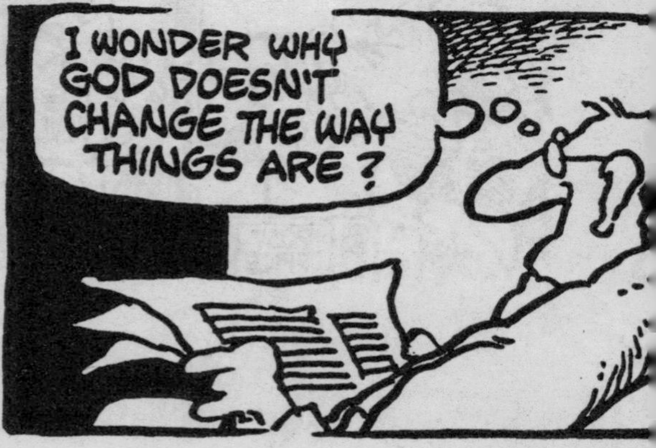
I WONDER WHY GOD DOESN'T CHANGE THE WAY THINGS ARE?

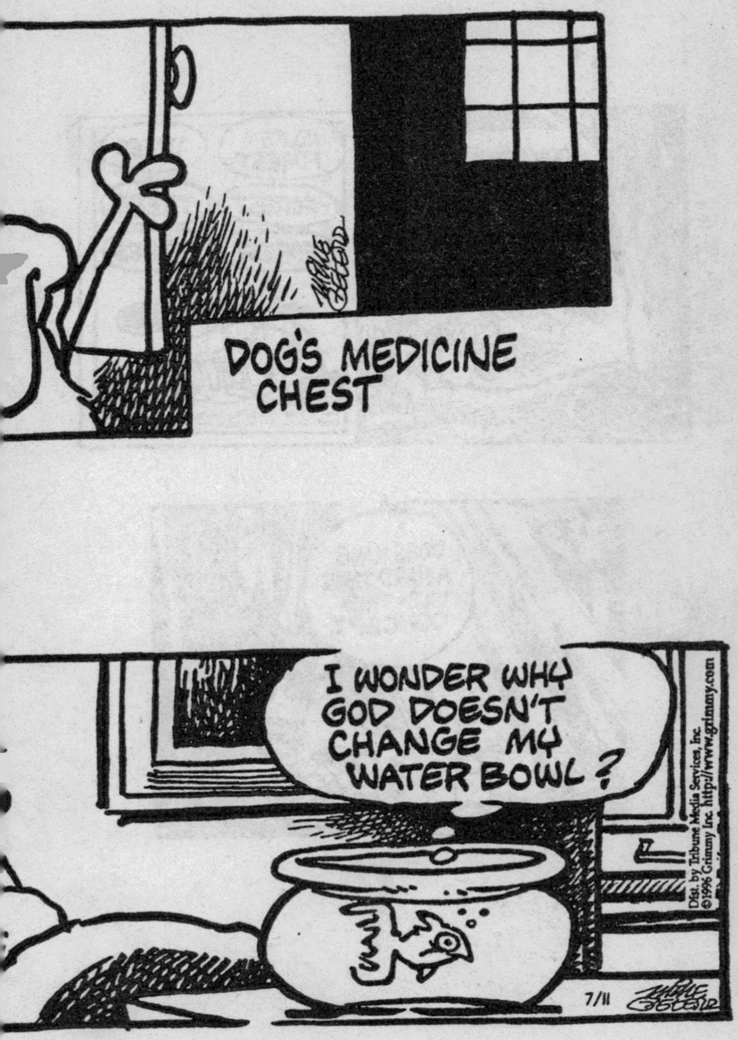
DOG'S MEDICINE CHEST
I WONDER WHY GOD DOESN'T CHANGE MY WATER BOWL?
Dist. by Tribune Media Services, Inc.
©1996 Grimmy Inc. http://www.grimmy.com
7/11

LOOK GRIMM, A FOREST.
NO, THEY'RE TREES
NO, IT'S A FOREST
TREES
FOREST
TREES
FOREST
TREES
Dist. by Tribune Media Services, Inc.
©1997 Grimmy, Inc. http://www.grimmy.com
DOGS HAVE A HARD TIME WITH THIS CONCEPT.
SNIFF SNIFF SNIFF

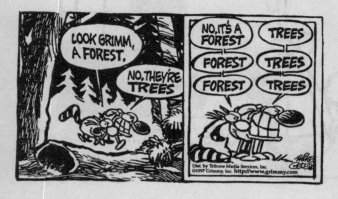

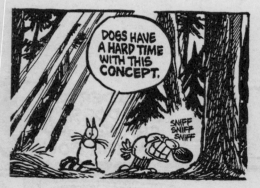

BOY, IT'S A BIG FOREST, BUT DON'T WORRY WE'RE NOT LOST...
I'VE BEEN DROPPING LITTLE KITTY TREATS BEHIND US, TO FIND OUR WAY BACK.
Dist. by Tribune Media Services, Inc.
©1997 Grimmy, Inc. http://www.grimmy.com
MEOW MEOW MEOW MEOW MEOW MEOW
NICE JOB, LEWIS AND CLARK.

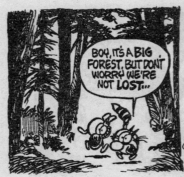

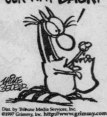

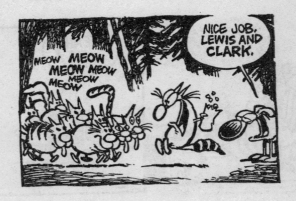

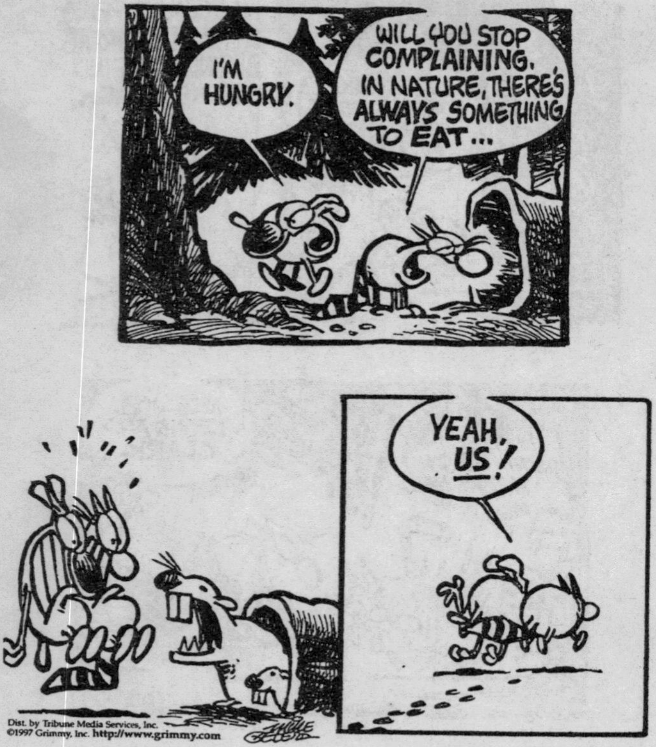
I'M HUNGRY.
WILL YOU STOP COMPLAINING. IN NATURE, THERE'S ALWAYS SOMETHING TO EAT...
YEAH, US!
Dist. by Tribune Media Services, Inc.
©1997 Grimmy, Inc. http://www.grimmy.com

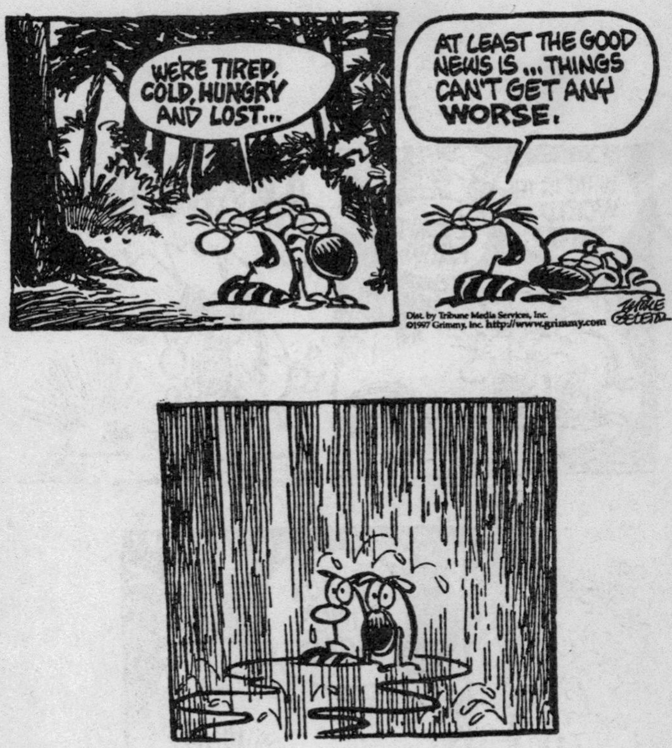
WE'RE TIRED, COLD, HUNGRY AND LOST...
AT LEAST THE GOOD NEWS IS ... THINGS CAN'T GET ANY WORSE.
Dist. by Tribune Media Services, Inc.
©1997 Grimmy, Inc. http://www.grimmy.com

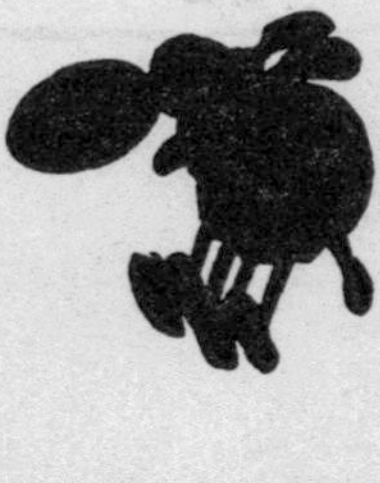

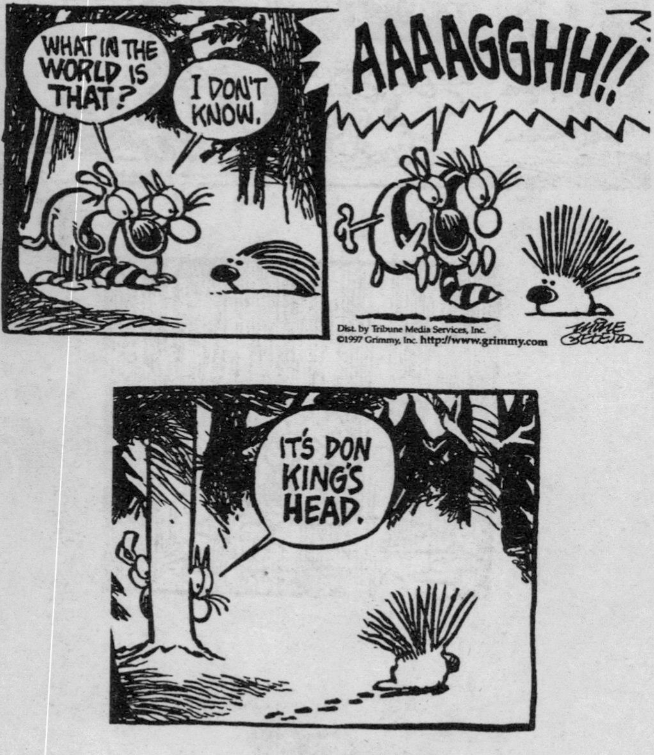
WHAT IN THE WORLD IS THAT?
I DON'T KNOW.
AAAAGGHH!!
Dist. by Tribune Media Services, Inc.
©1997 Grimmy, Inc. http://www.grimmy.com
IT'S DON KING'S HEAD.

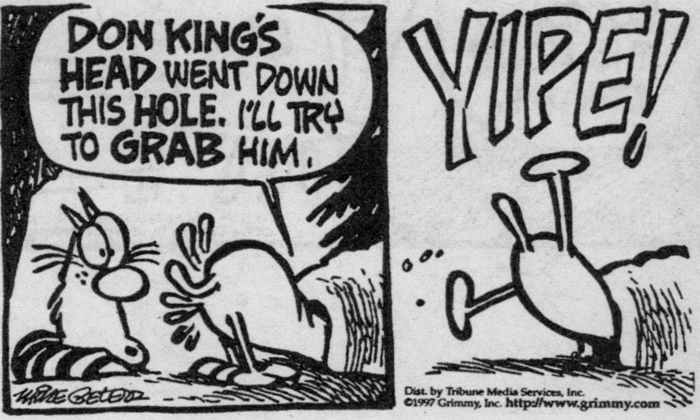
DON KING'S HEAD WENT DOWN THIS HOLE. I'LL TRY TO GRAB HIM.
YIPE!
Dist. by Tribune Media Services, Inc.
©1997 Grimmy, Inc. http://www.grimmy.com

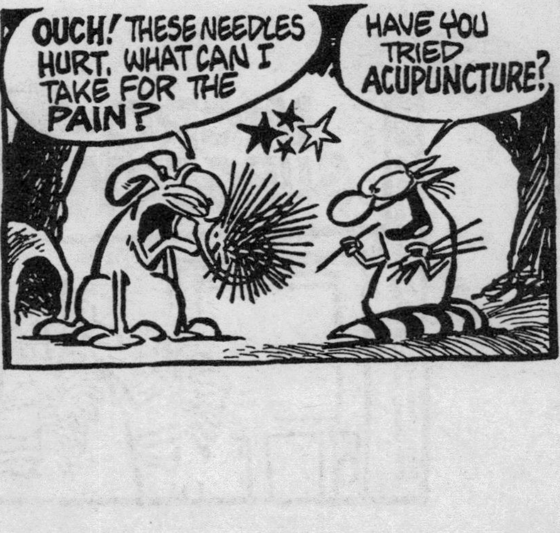
OUCH! THESE NEEDLES HURT. WHAT CAN I TAKE FOR THE PAIN?
HAVE YOU TRIED ACUPUNCTURE?

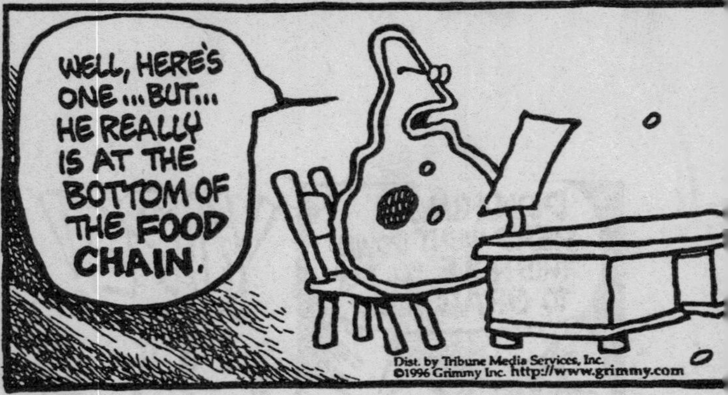
WELL, HERE'S ONE ... BUT... HE REALLY IS AT THE BOTTOM OF THE FOOD CHAIN.
Dist. by Tribune Media Services, Inc.
©1996 Grimmy Inc. http://www.grimmy.com

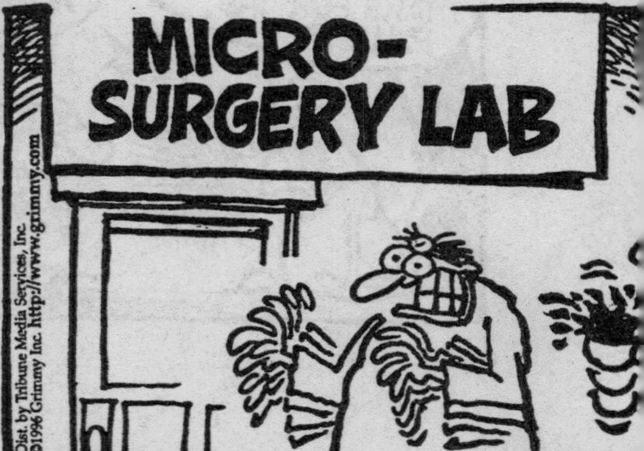
MICRO-SURGERY LAB
Dist. by Tribune Media Services, Inc.
©1996 Grimmy Inc. http://www.grimmy.com

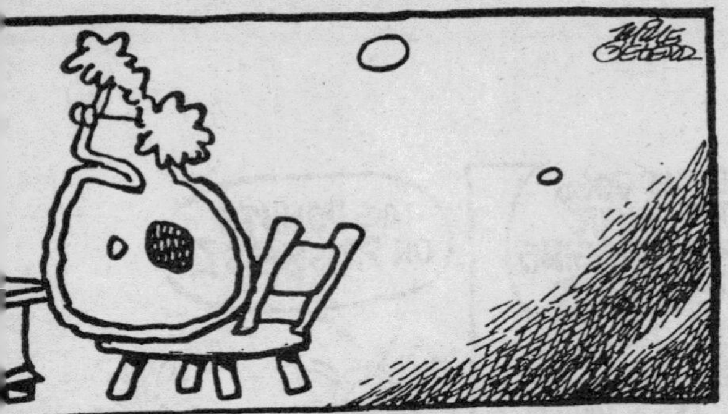

AMOEBA DATING SERVICES

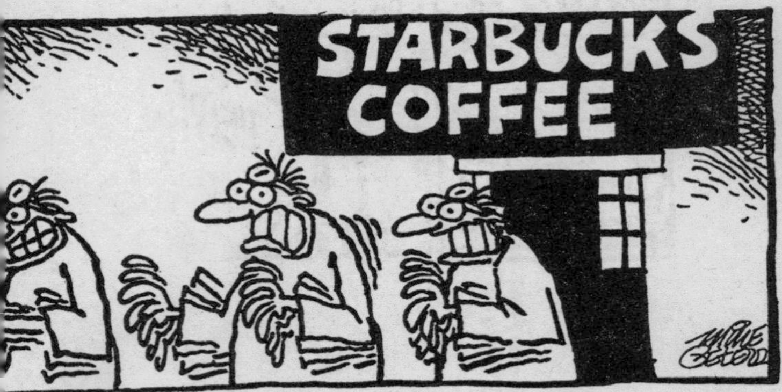
STARBUCKS
COFFEE

EVENTUALLY THE LAB WAS FORCED TO MOVE

IS IT TRUE THAT DOGS CAN'T STOP THEIR TAILS FROM WAGGING WHEN THEY HEAR GOOD THINGS?
I GUESS, WHY?
LIKE DONUTS OR FRISBEES?..
HEY!
..OR PORK CHOPS OR ICE CREAM?
...OR TWINKIES OR....
HELP!
Dist. by Tribune Media Services, Inc. ©1997 Grimmy, Inc. http://www.grimmy.com

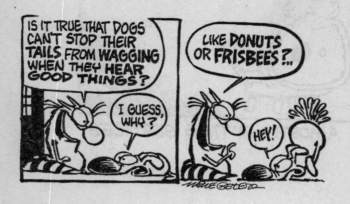

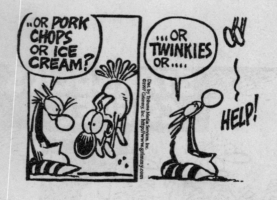

GRIMMY, YOU'RE WAGGING YOUR TAIL SO FAST YOU'RE FLYING!
KEEP IT UP... NOTHING CAN STOP YOU NOW!
Dist. by Tribune Media Services, Inc.
©1997 Grimmy, Inc. http://www.grimmy.com
BONK BONK BONK BONK
...EXCEPT FOR THAT CEILING FAN.

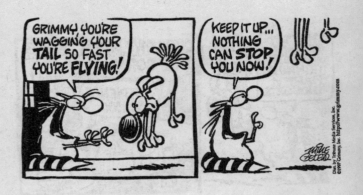

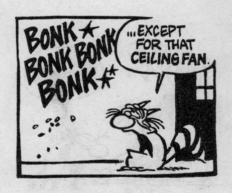

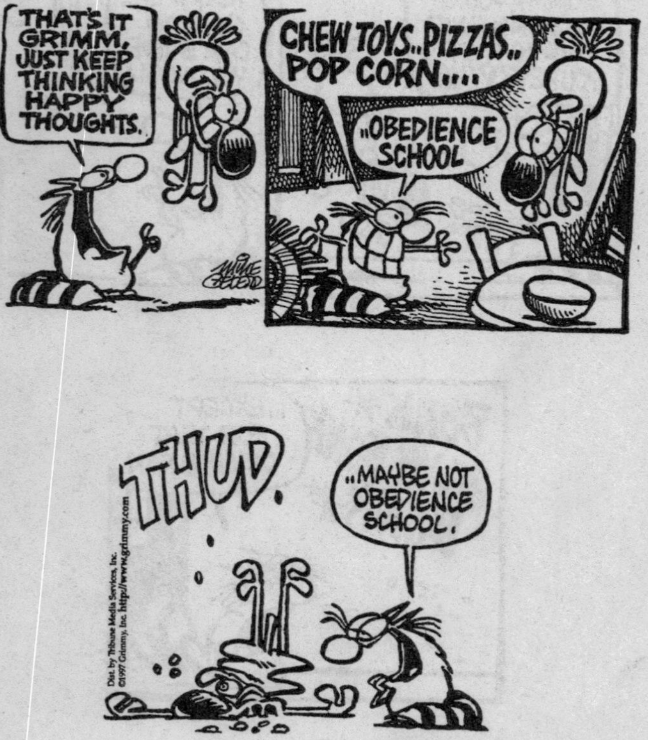

THAT'S IT GRIMM, JUST KEEP THINKING HAPPY THOUGHTS.
CHEW TOYS..PIZZAS.. POP CORN....
..OBEDIENCE SCHOOL
THUD.
..MAYBE NOT OBEDIENCE SCHOOL.
Dist by Tribune Media Services, Inc.
©1997 Grimmy, Inc http://www.grimmy.com

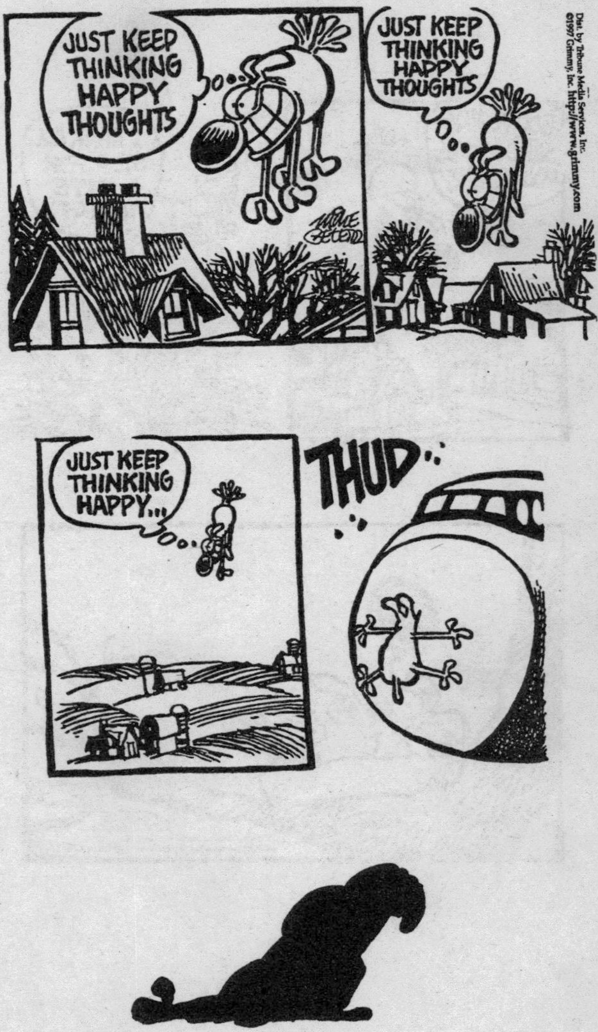
JUST KEEP THINKING HAPPY THOUGHTS
JUST KEEP THINKING HAPPY THOUGHTS
Dist. by Tribune Media Services, Inc. ©1997 Grimmy, Inc. http://www.grimmy.com
JUST KEEP THINKING HAPPY...
THUD

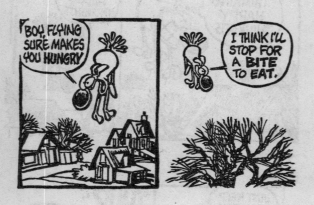

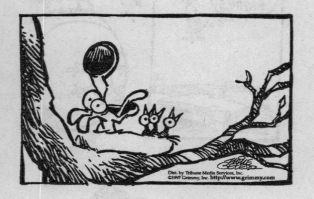

BOY, FLYING SURE MAKES YOU HUNGRY
I THINK I'LL STOP FOR A BITE TO EAT.
Dist. by Tribune Media Services, Inc.
©1997 Grimmy, Inc. http://www.grimmy.com

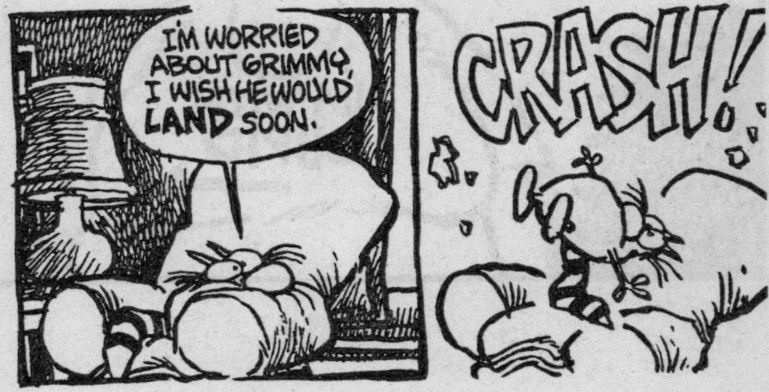
I'M WORRIED ABOUT GRIMMY, I WISH HE WOULD LAND SOON.
CRASH!

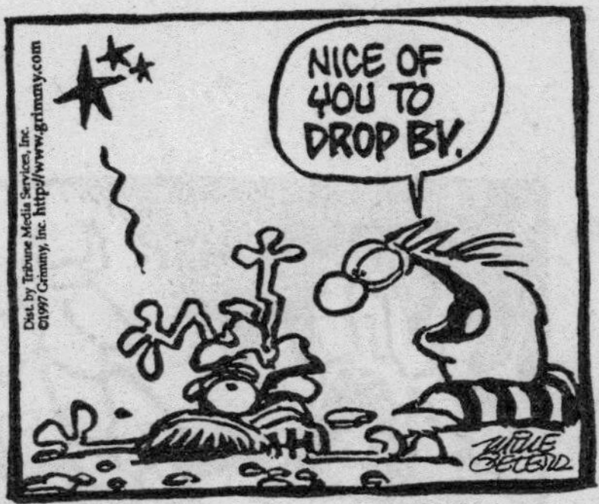
Dist. by Tribune Media Services, Inc.
©1997 Grimmy, Inc. http://www.grimmy.com
NICE OF YOU TO DROP BY.

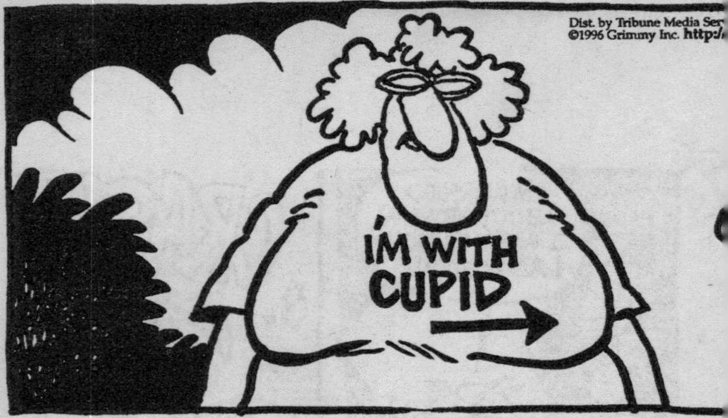
Dist. by Tribune Media Ser
©1996 Grimmy Inc. http:/
IM WITH
CUPID

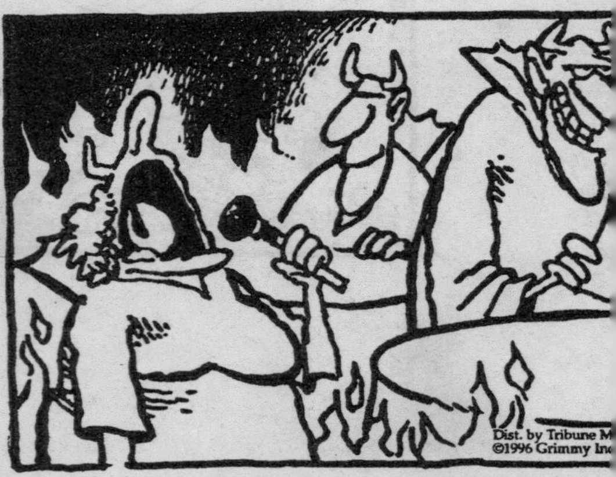
Dist. by Tribune M
©1996 Grimmy In

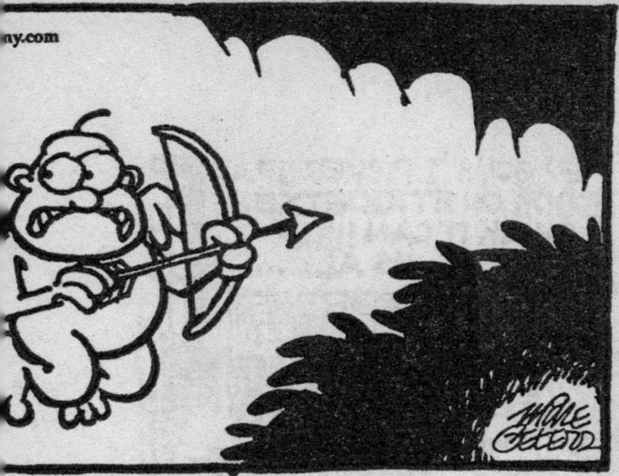

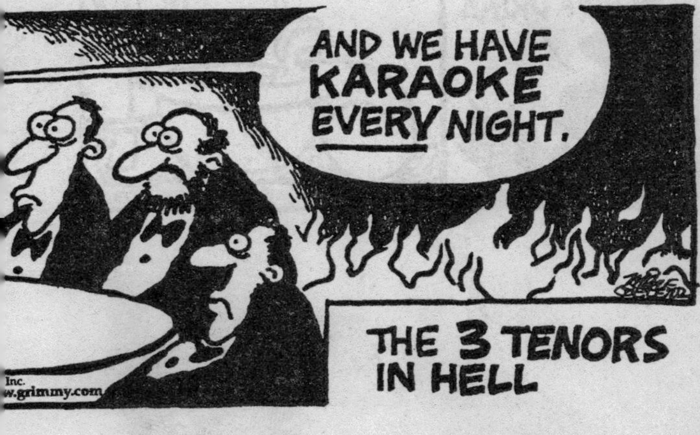
AND WE HAVE KARAOKE EVERY NIGHT.

THE 3 TENORS IN HELL

HEY GUYS, I PICKED UP A BOOK ON ETIQUETTE. I THINK IT CAN HELP US ALL...
Dist. by Tribune Media Services, Inc.
©1998 Grimmy Inc. http://www.grimmy.com

IT SAYS HERE THAT IT SHOWS CLASS TO EXTEND A PINKY WHEN TAKING A DRINK

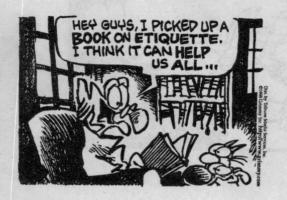

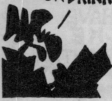

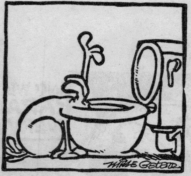

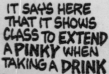

GIVE ME YOUR FOOD.
GRIMM... IT'S POLITE TO USE THE WORD "MAY" WHEN YOU ASK FOR SOMETHING.
GIVE ME YOUR FOOD OR I MAY KILL YOU.
Dist. by Tribune Media Services, Inc. ©1998 Grimmy Inc. http://www.grimmy.com

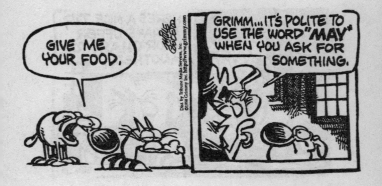

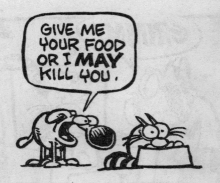

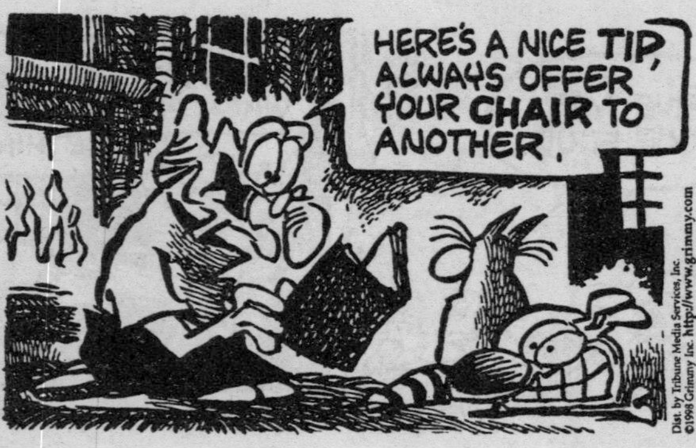
HERE'S A NICE TIP, ALWAYS OFFER YOUR CHAIR TO ANOTHER.
Dist. by Tribune Media Services, Inc.
©1998 Grimmy Inc. http://www.grimmy.com

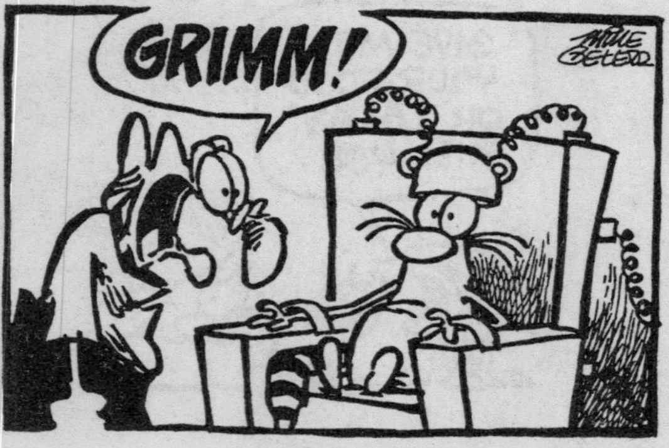
GRIMM!

GRIMM, JUST ONCE CAN'T YOU EAT YOUR FOOD SO I CAN'T HEAR YOU?
CRUNCH
MUNCH
CHEW
GULP
Dist. by Tribune Media Services, Inc.
©1998 Grimmy Inc. http://www.grimmy.com

SLAM
CHEW
CRUNCH
CHOMP
GULP

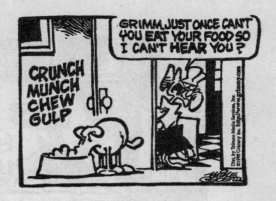

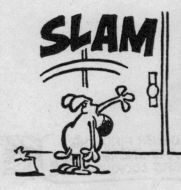

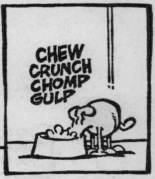

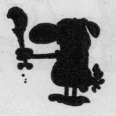

Dist. by Tribune Media Services, Inc.
©1998 Grimmy Inc. http://www.grimmy.com

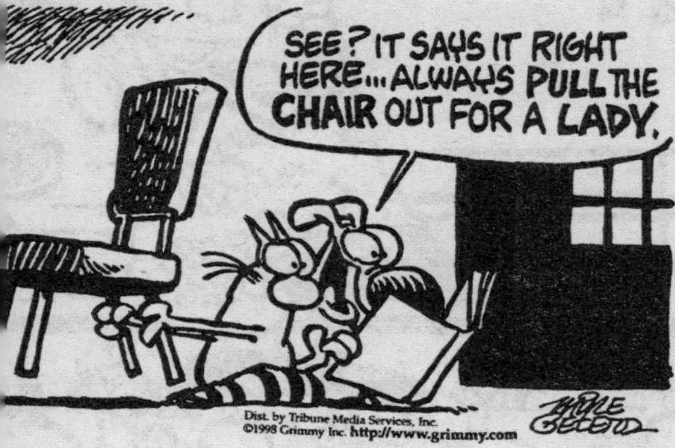
SEE? IT SAYS IT RIGHT HERE... ALWAYS PULL THE CHAIR OUT FOR A LADY.
Dist. by Tribune Media Services, Inc.
©1998 Grimmy Inc. http://www.grimmy.com

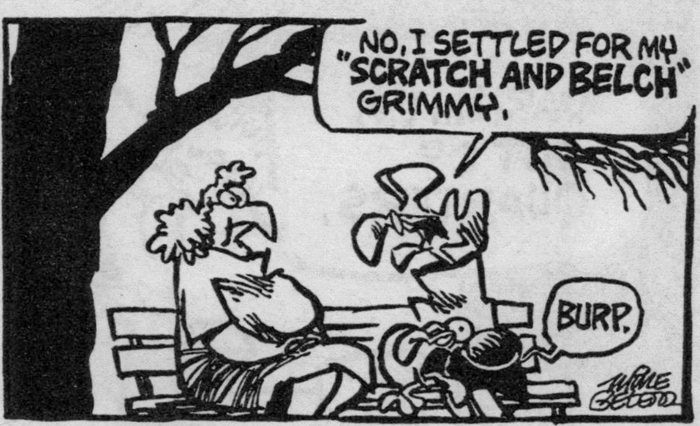
...NO, I SETTLED FOR MY "SCRATCH AND BELCH" GRIMMY.
BURP.

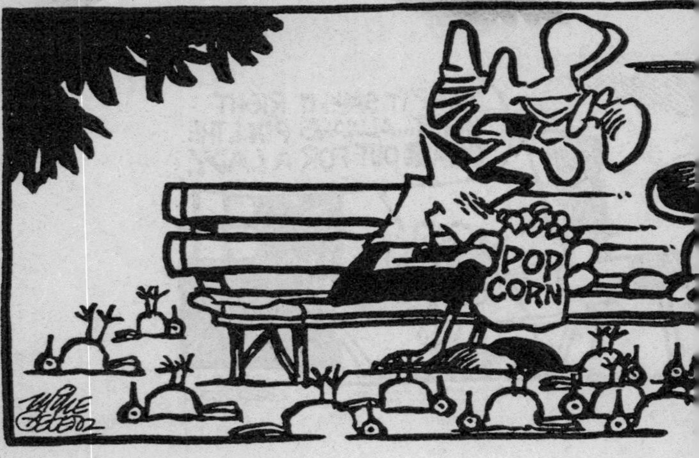
POP
CORN

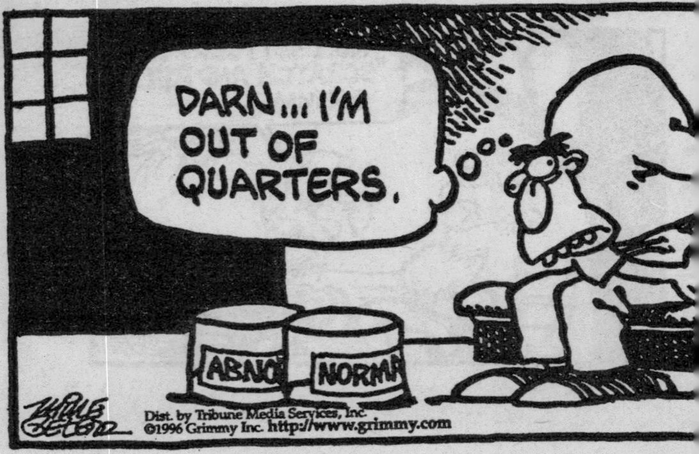
DARN... I'M
OUT OF
QUARTERS.
ABNO
NORM
Dist. by Tribune Media Services, Inc.
©1996 Grimmy Inc. http://www.grimmy.com

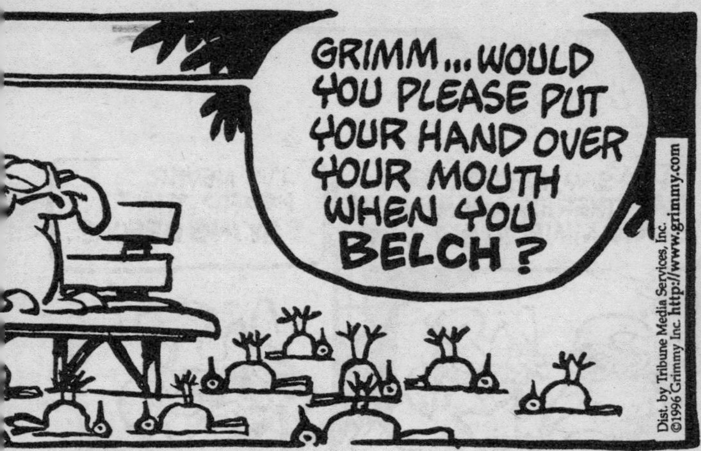
GRIMM... WOULD YOU PLEASE PUT YOUR HAND OVER YOUR MOUTH WHEN YOU BELCH?
Dist. by Tribune Media Services, Inc.
©1996 Grimmy Inc. http://www.grimmy.com

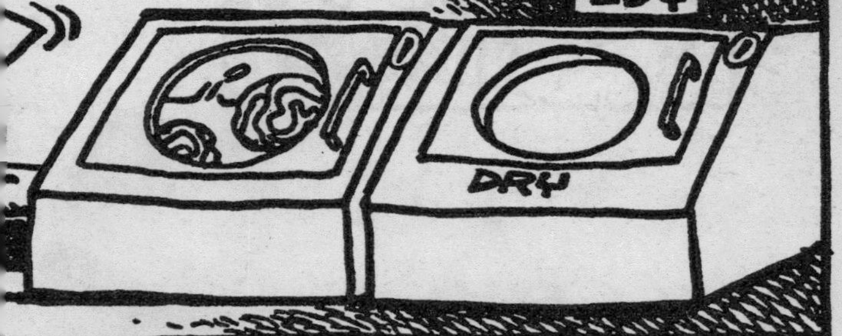
BRAINWASHING
25¢
DRY

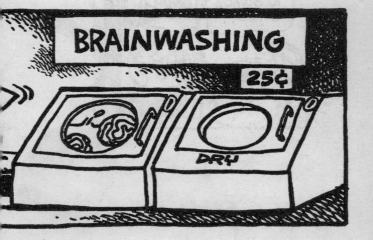

THEY SAY, INSIDE EVERY CAT THERE'S A MAILMAN SCREAMING TO GET OUT.
I'VE NEVER HEARD THAT SAYING BEFORE.
Dist. by Tribune Media Services, Inc. ©1998 Grimmy Inc. http://www.grimmy.com
..OBVIOUSLY YOU HAVEN'T LISTENED TO SUMO'S STOMACH LATELY.

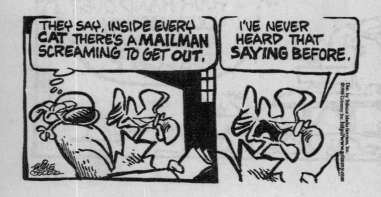

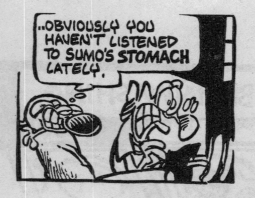

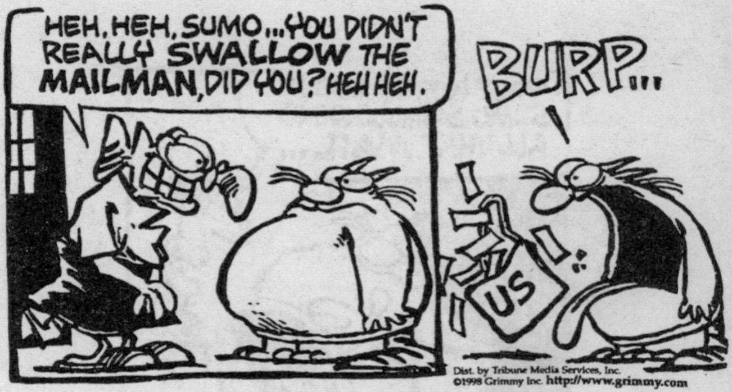
HEH, HEH, SUMO...YOU DIDN'T REALLY SWALLOW THE MAILMAN, DID YOU? HEH HEH.
BURP...
US
Dist. by Tribune Media Services, Inc.
©1998 Grimmy Inc. http://www.grimmy.com

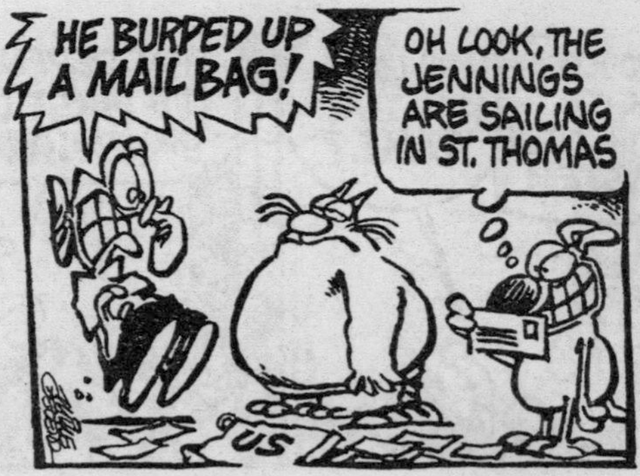
HE BURPED UP A MAIL BAG!
OH LOOK, THE JENNINGS ARE SAILING IN ST. THOMAS
US

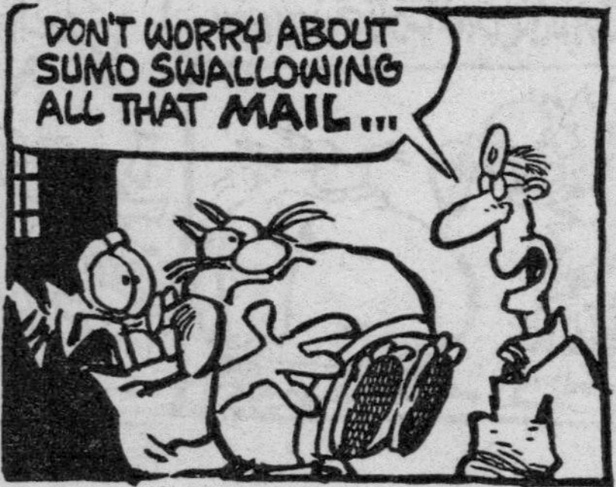
DON'T WORRY ABOUT SUMO SWALLOWING ALL THAT MAIL...

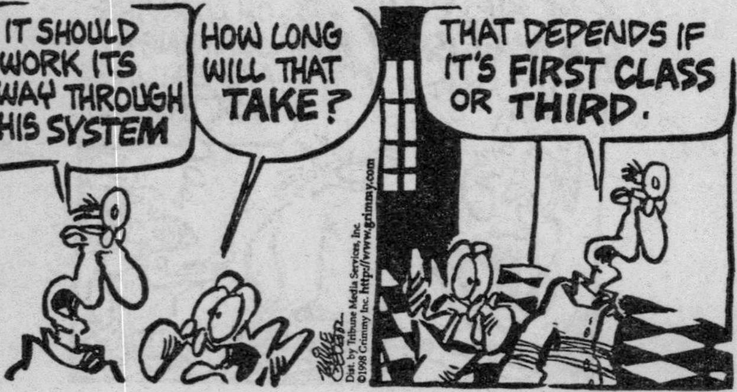
IT SHOULD WORK ITS WAY THROUGH HIS SYSTEM
HOW LONG WILL THAT TAKE?
THAT DEPENDS IF IT'S FIRST CLASS OR THIRD.
Dist. by Tribune Media Services, Inc.
©1998 Grimmy Inc. http://www.grimmy.com

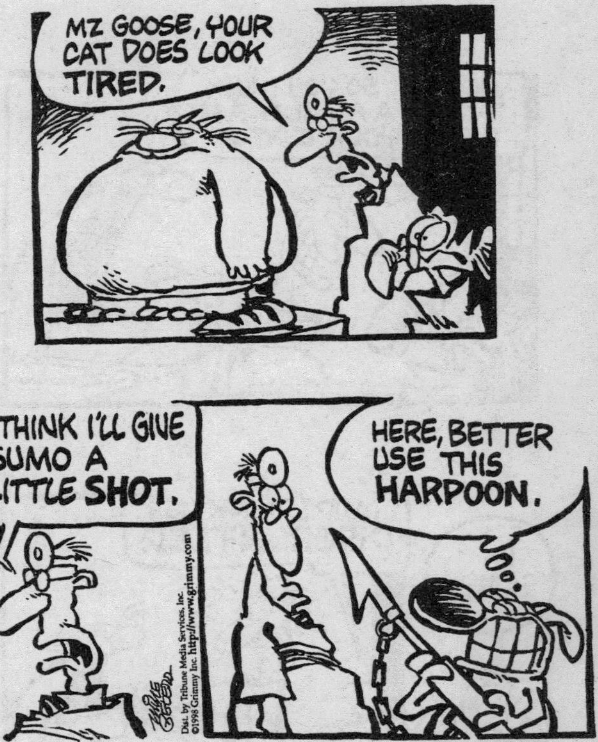
MZ GOOSE, YOUR CAT DOES LOOK TIRED.
I THINK I'LL GIVE SUMO A LITTLE SHOT.
HERE, BETTER USE THIS HARPOON.
Dist. by Tribune Media Services, Inc.
©1998 Grimmy Inc. http://www.grimmy.com

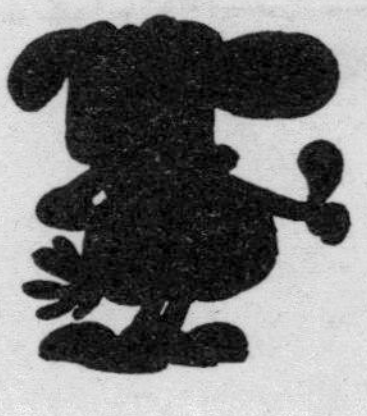

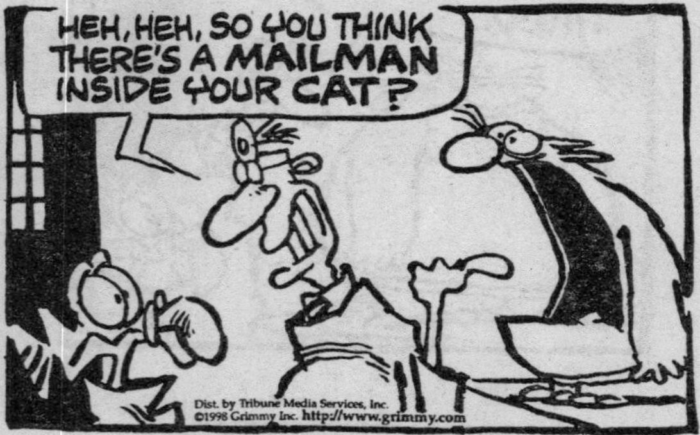
HEH, HEH, SO YOU THINK THERE'S A MAILMAN INSIDE YOUR CAT?
Dist. by Tribune Media Services, Inc.
©1998 Grimmy Inc. http://www.grimmy.com

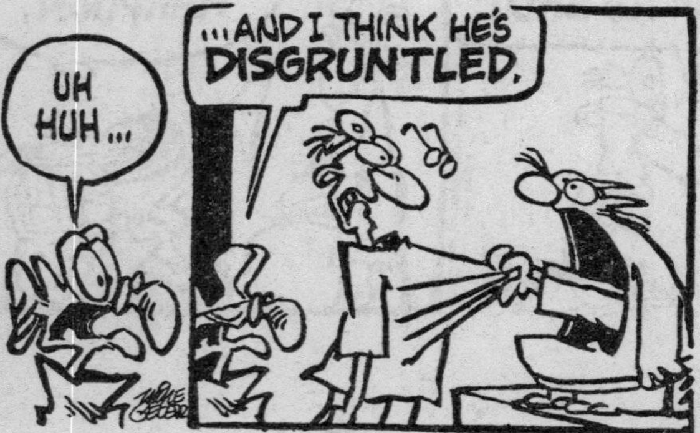
UH HUH...
...AND I THINK HE'S DISGRUNTLED.

OK, LET'S TRY THE HEIMLICH. ONE, TWO, THREE...
Dist. by Tribune Media Services, Inc. ©1998 Grimmy Inc. http://www.grimmy.com
SQUEEZE
POP...

GEE, IT WAS THE MAILMAN!
WE'D BETTER RUN BEFORE HE GOES POSTAL!

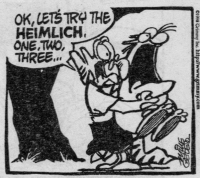

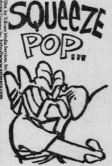

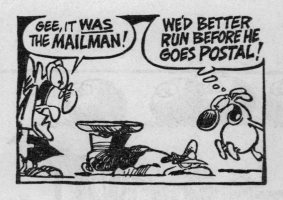

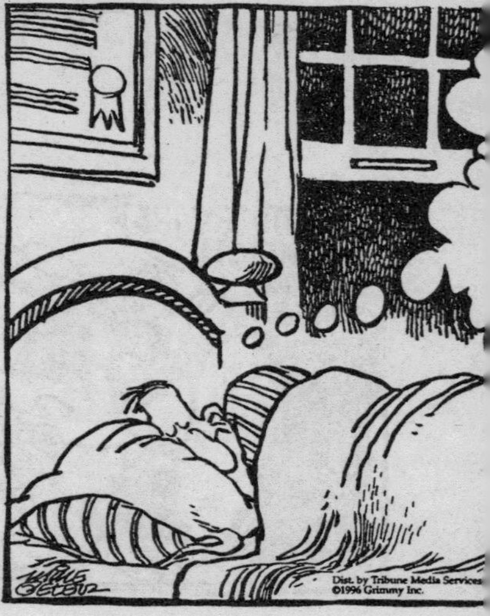
Dist. by Tribune Media Services
©1996 Grimmy Inc.

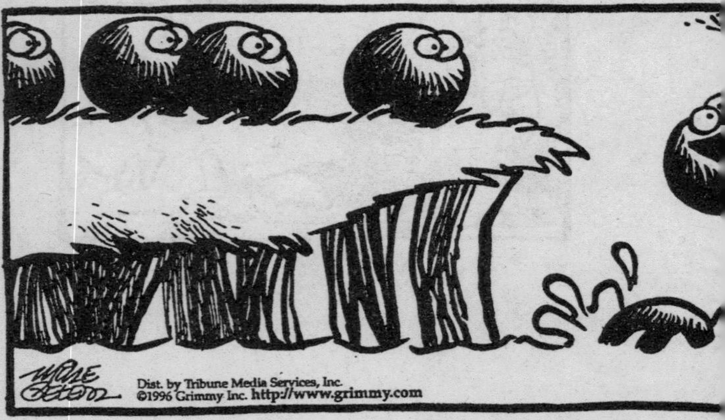
Dist. by Tribune Media Services, Inc.
©1996 Grimmy Inc. http://www.grimmy.com

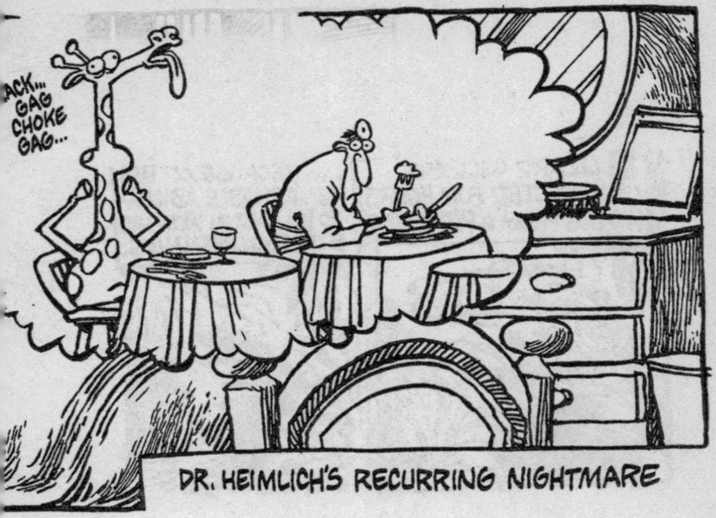
ACK... GAG CHOKE GAG...

DR. HEIMLICH'S RECURRING NIGHTMARE

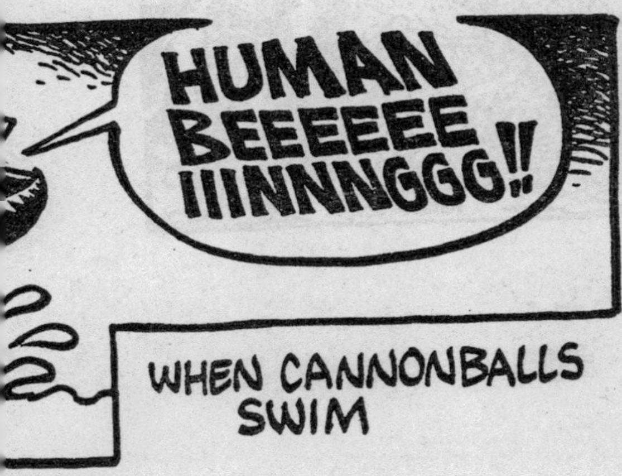
HUMAN BEEEEEE IIINNNGGG!!

WHEN CANNONBALLS SWIM

A LIZARD WILL SIT UNDETECTED FOR HOURS, HIDING FROM A PREDATOR.
Dist. by Tribune Media Services, Inc. ©1998 Grimmy Inc. http://www.grimmy.com
.....BECAUSE OF HIS REMARKABLE ABILITY TO BLEND IN WITH HIS SURROUNDINGS.
GRIMM, TAKE OFF THAT HAWAIIAN SHIRT. WE'RE GOING TO THE VET
MIKE PETERS

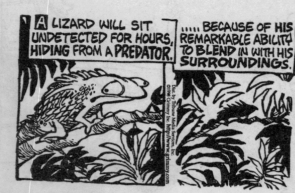

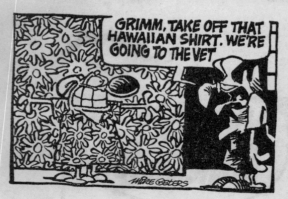

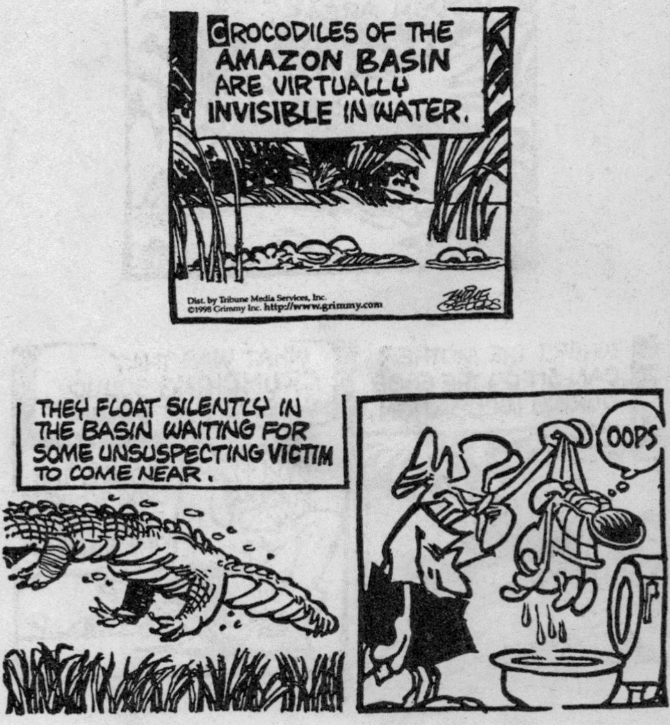
CROCODILES OF THE AMAZON BASIN ARE VIRTUALLY INVISIBLE IN WATER.
Dist. by Tribune Media Services, Inc.
©1998 Grimmy Inc. http://www.grimmy.com
THEY FLOAT SILENTLY IN THE BASIN WAITING FOR SOME UNSUSPECTING VICTIM TO COME NEAR.
OOPS

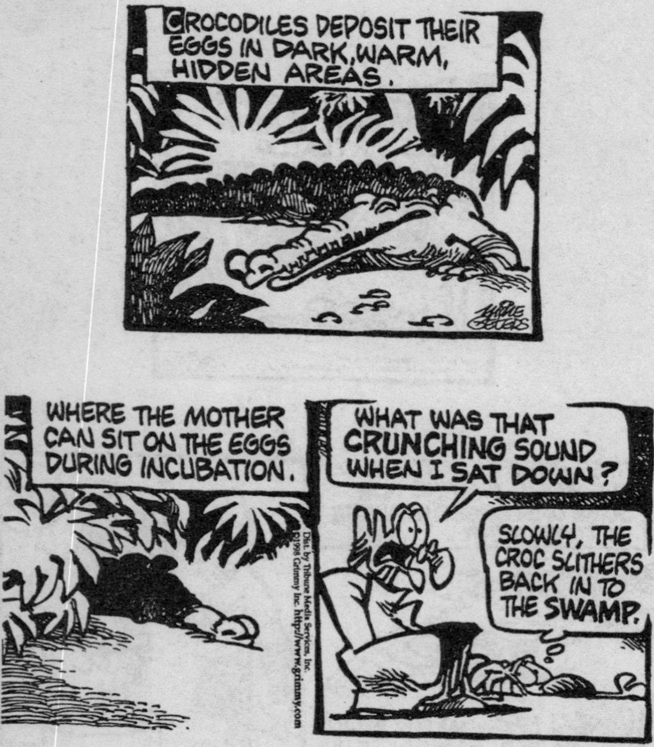
CROCODILES DEPOSIT THEIR EGGS IN DARK, WARM, HIDDEN AREAS.
WHERE THE MOTHER CAN SIT ON THE EGGS DURING INCUBATION.
Dist. by Tribune Media Services, Inc. ©1998 Grimmy Inc. http://www.grimmy.com
WHAT WAS THAT CRUNCHING SOUND WHEN I SAT DOWN?
SLOWLY, THE CROC SLITHERS BACK IN TO THE SWAMP.

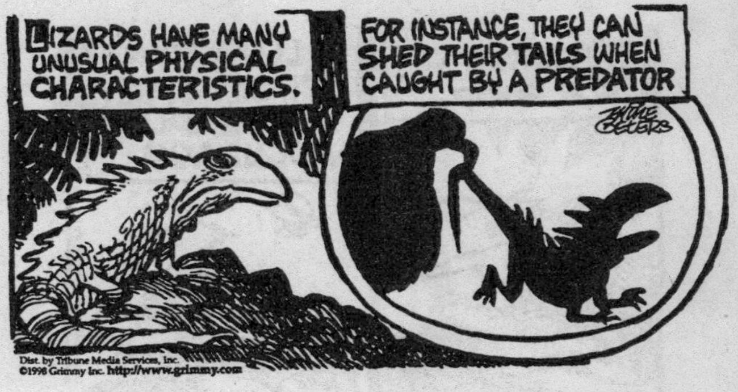
LIZARDS HAVE MANY UNUSUAL PHYSICAL CHARACTERISTICS.
FOR INSTANCE, THEY CAN SHED THEIR TAILS WHEN CAUGHT BY A PREDATOR
Dist. by Tribune Media Services, Inc.
©1998 Grimmy Inc. http://www.grimmy.com

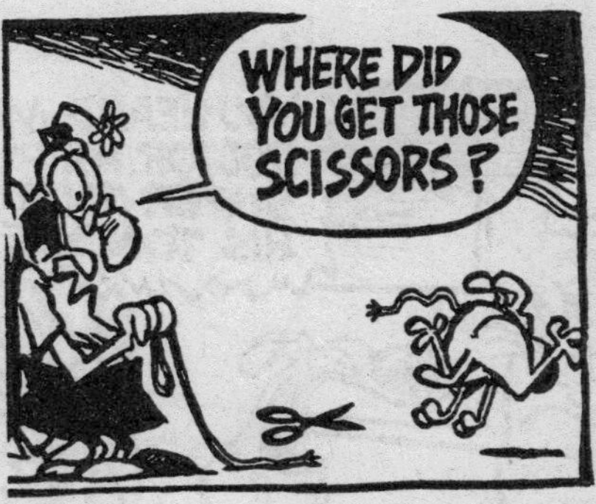
WHERE DID YOU GET THOSE SCISSORS?

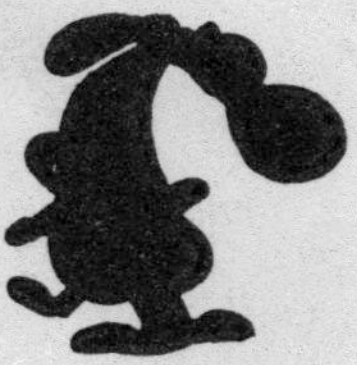

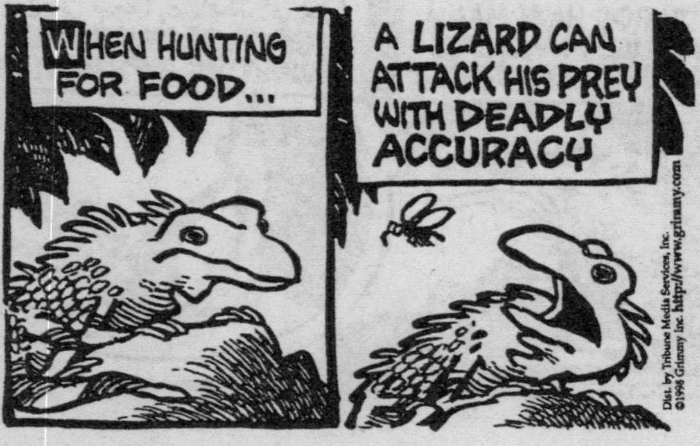
WHEN HUNTING FOR FOOD...
A LIZARD CAN ATTACK HIS PREY WITH DEADLY ACCURACY
Dist. by Tribune Media Services, Inc.
©1998 Grimmy Inc. http://www.grimmy.com

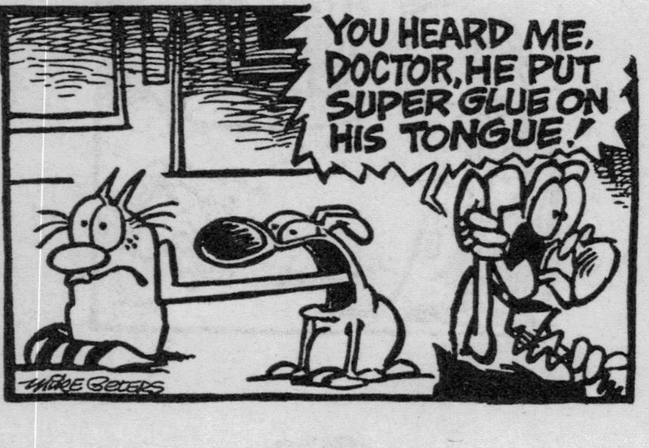
YOU HEARD ME, DOCTOR, HE PUT SUPER GLUE ON HIS TONGUE!
MIKE PETERS

SO YOU SAY YOUR DOG PUT SUPER GLUE ON HIS TONGUE...
...BECAUSE HE THOUGHT HE WAS A REPTILE?
HE'LL BE FINE, BUT FEED HIM LOTS OF INSECTS.
JUTHT UNTHTICK ME, THTUPID!
Dist. by Tribune Media Services, Inc.
©1998 Grimmy Inc. http://www.grimmy.com

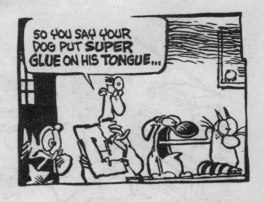

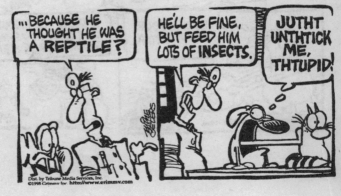

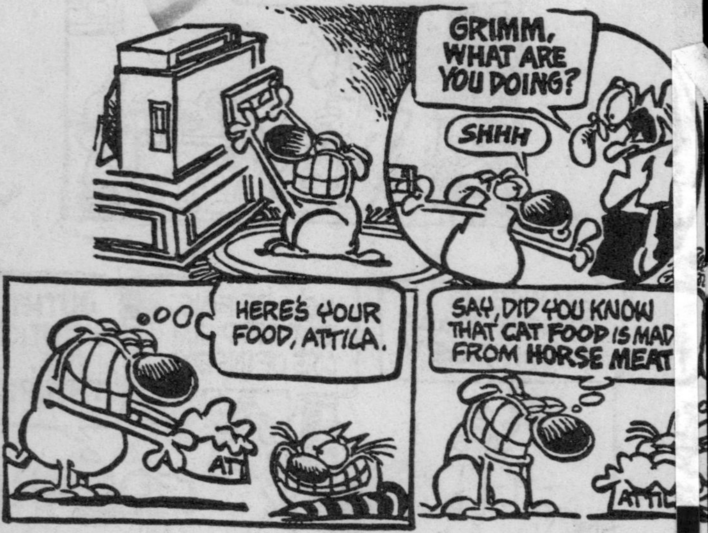
GRIMM, WHAT ARE YOU DOING?
SHHH
HERE'S YOUR FOOD, ATTILA.
AT
SAY, DID YOU KNOW THAT CAT FOOD IS MAD
FROM HORSE MEAT
ATTIL

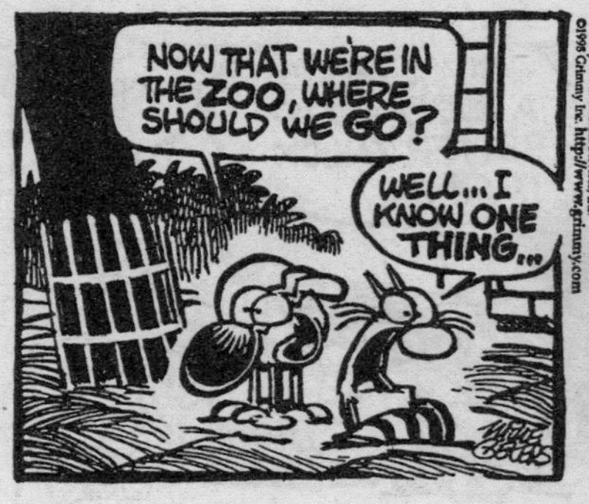
NOW THAT WE'RE IN THE ZOO, WHERE SHOULD WE GO?
WELL... I KNOW ONE THING...
Dist. by Tribune Media Services, Inc.
©1998 Grimmy Inc. http://www.grimmy.com

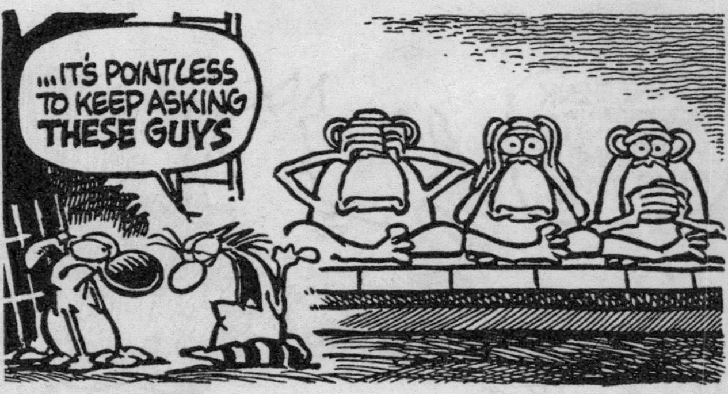
...IT'S POINTLESS TO KEEP ASKING THESE GUYS

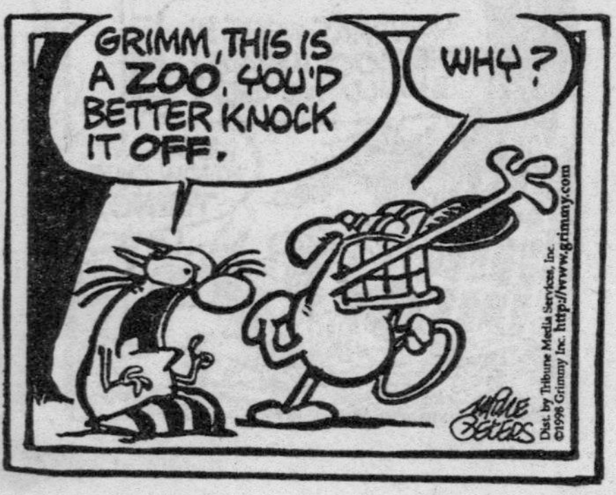
GRIMM, THIS IS A ZOO. YOU'D BETTER KNOCK IT OFF.
WHY?
MIKE PETERS
Dist. by Tribune Media Services, Inc.
©1998 Grimmy Inc. http://www.grimmy.com

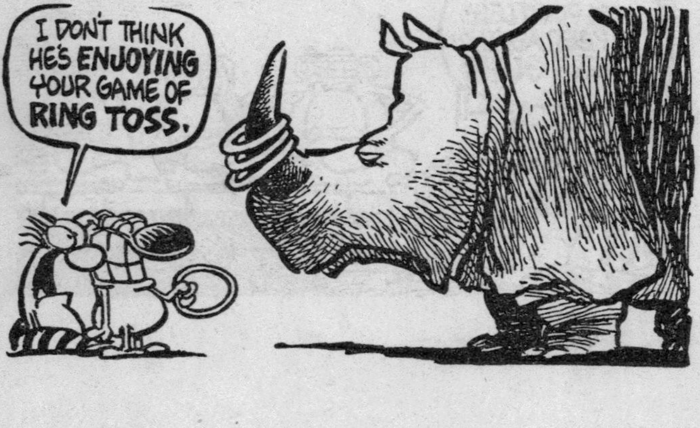
I DON'T THINK HE'S ENJOYING YOUR GAME OF RING TOSS.

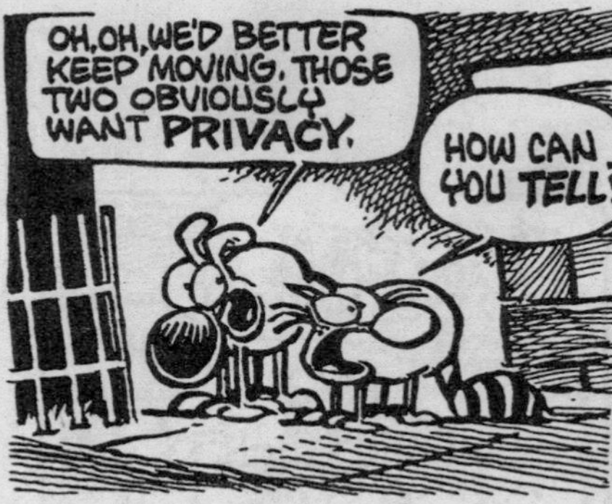
OH, OH, WE'D BETTER KEEP MOVING. THOSE TWO OBVIOUSLY WANT **PRIVACY**.
HOW CAN YOU **TELL**?

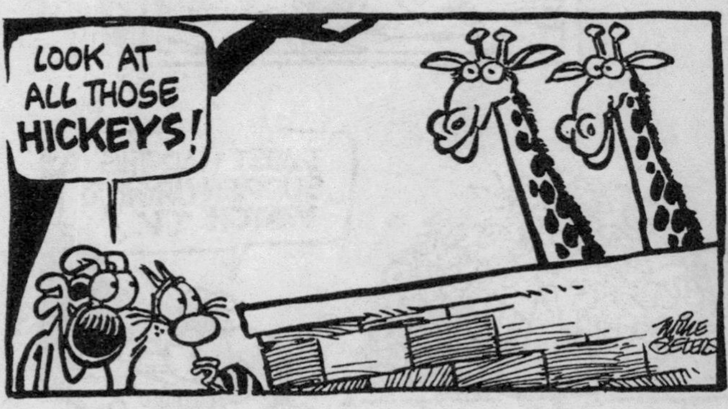
LOOK AT ALL THOSE **HICKEYS**!

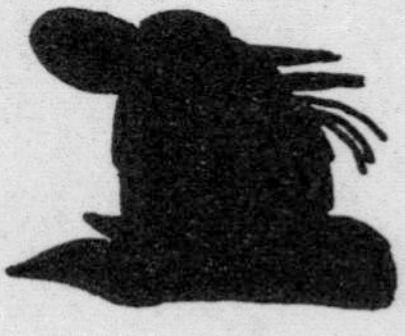

IT'S FUN HERE AT THE ZOO, BUT WE NEED TO GO HOME.
WHY?
I JUST HAD THIS SUDDEN URGE TO WATCH T.V.!
Dist. by Tribune Media Services, Inc.
©1998 Grimmy Inc. http://www.grimmy.com

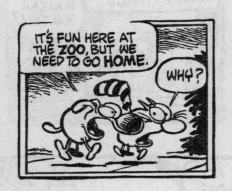

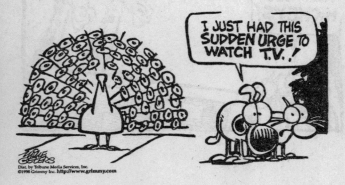

SNIFF
SNIFF
DON'T EVEN THINK ABOUT IT.

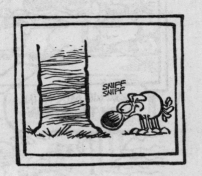

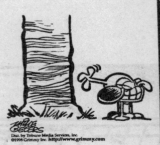

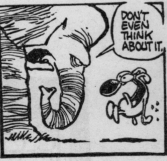

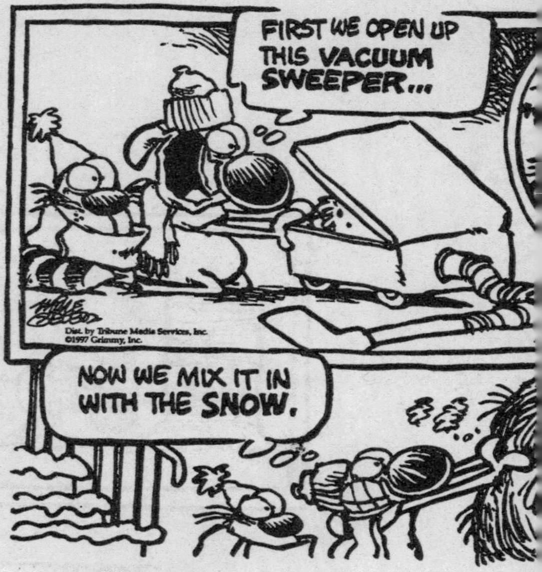
FIRST WE OPEN UP THIS VACUUM SWEEPER...
Dist. by Tribune Media Services, Inc. ©1997 Grimmy, Inc.
NOW WE MIX IT IN WITH THE SNOW.

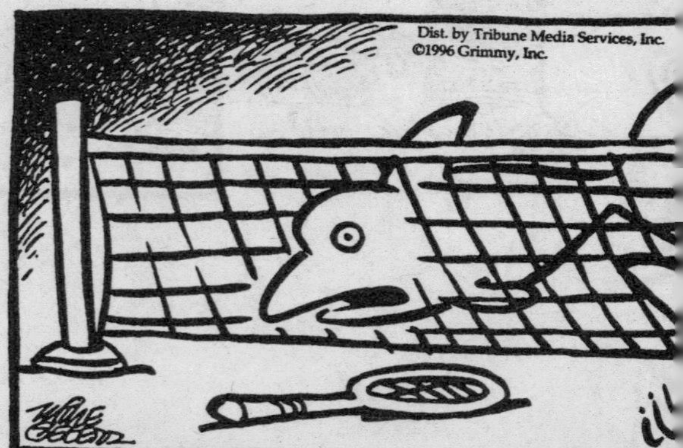
Dist. by Tribune Media Services, Inc.
©1996 Grimmy, Inc.

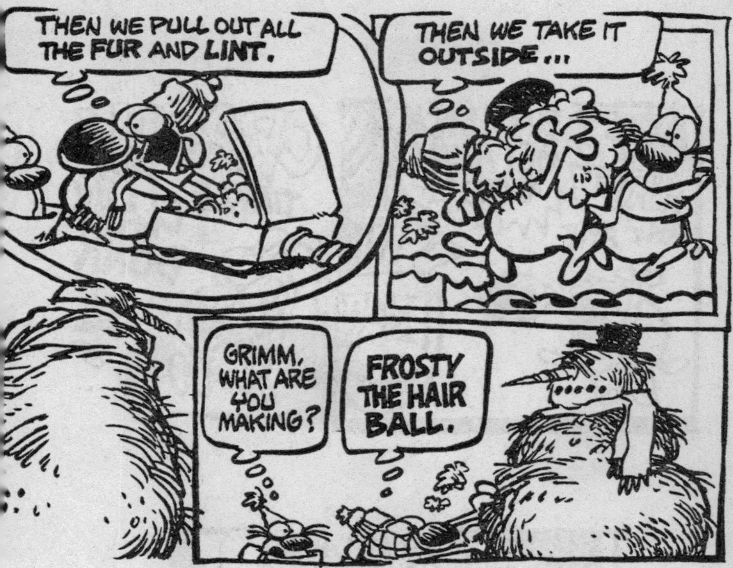
THEN WE PULL OUT ALL THE FUR AND LINT.
THEN WE TAKE IT OUTSIDE...
GRIMM, WHAT ARE YOU MAKING?
FROSTY THE HAIR BALL.

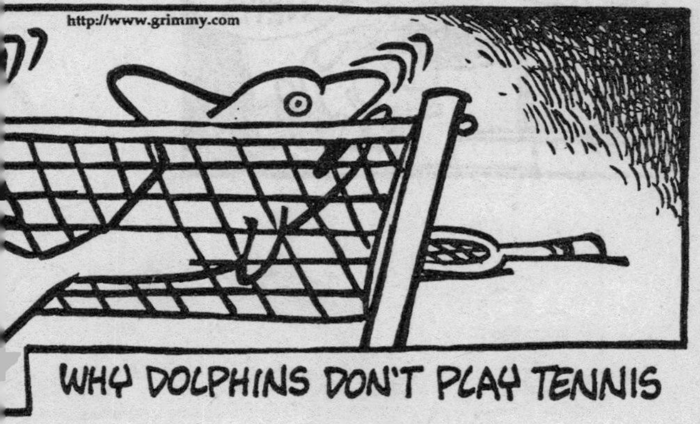
http://www.grimmy.com
WHY DOLPHINS DON'T PLAY TENNIS

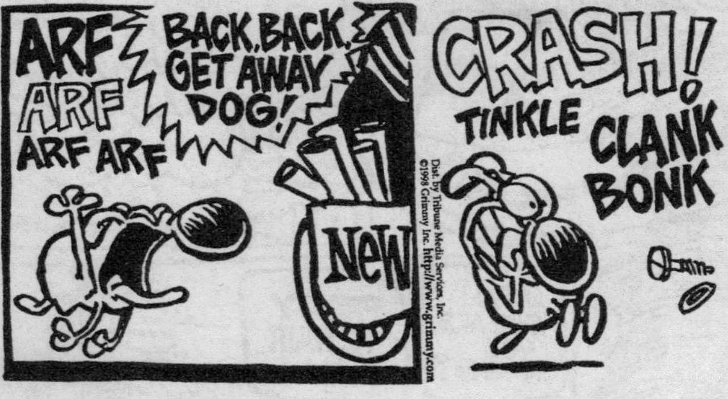
ARF
ARF
ARF ARF
BACK, BACK, GET AWAY DOG!
New
Dist. by Tribune Media Services, Inc. ©1998 Grimmy Inc. http://www.grimmy.com
CRASH!
TINKLE
CLANK
BONK

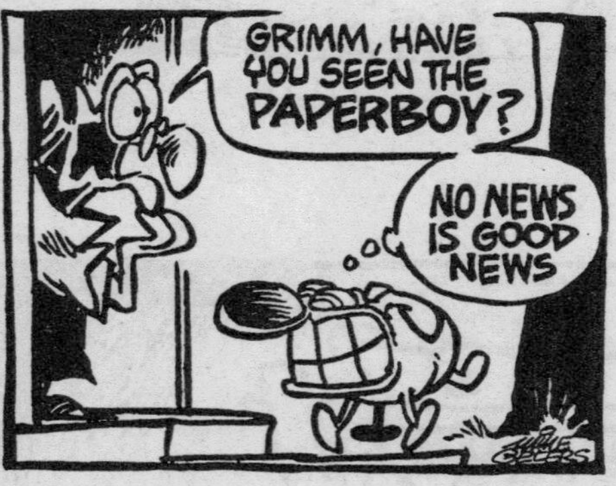
GRIMM, HAVE YOU SEEN THE PAPERBOY?
NO NEWS IS GOOD NEWS
MIKE PETERS

HERE COMES THAT PAPERBOY AGAIN.
I'LL CATCH WHATEVER HE THROWS AT ME.
MIKE PETERS
Dist. by Tribune Media Services, Inc.
©1998 Grimmy Inc. http://www.grimmy.com
WHAP!
THIS IS WHY JOURNALISTS RANK SO LOW IN OPINION POLLS.

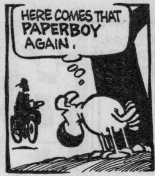

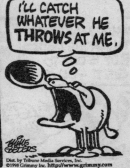

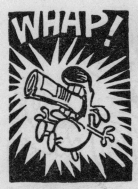

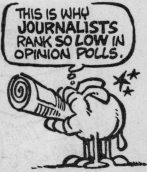

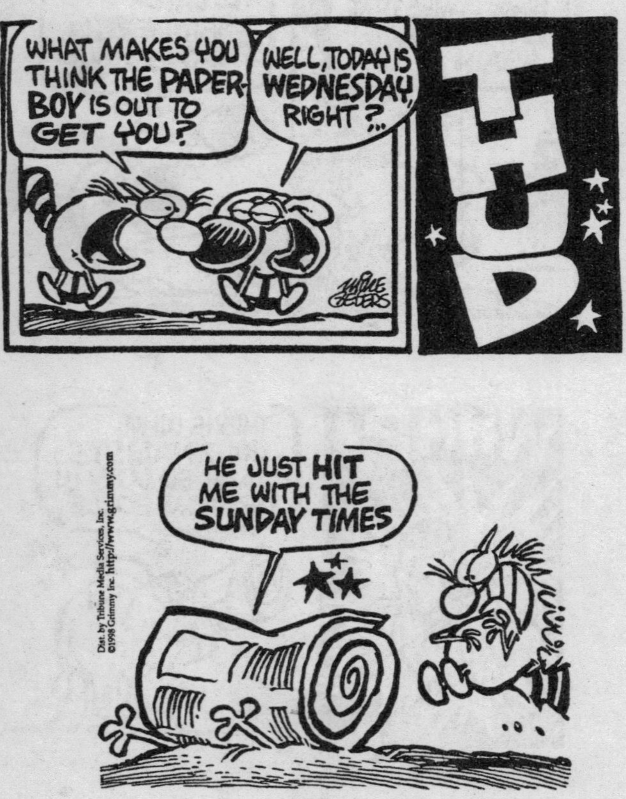
WHAT MAKES YOU THINK THE PAPER-BOY IS OUT TO GET YOU?
WELL, TODAY IS WEDNESDAY, RIGHT?...
MIKE PETERS
THUD
HE JUST HIT ME WITH THE SUNDAY TIMES
Dist. by Tribune Media Services, Inc.
©1998 Grimmy Inc. http://www.grimmy.com

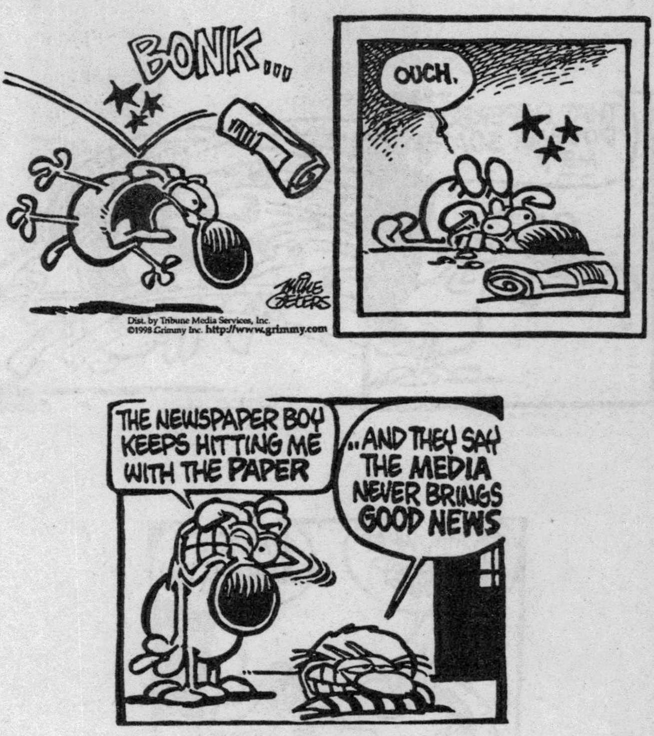
BONK...
OUCH.
THE NEWSPAPER BOY KEEPS HITTING ME WITH THE PAPER
...AND THEY SAY THE MEDIA NEVER BRINGS GOOD NEWS
MIKE PETERS
Dist. by Tribune Media Services, Inc.
©1998 Grimmy Inc. http://www.grimmy.com

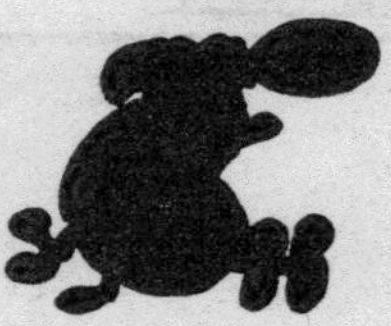

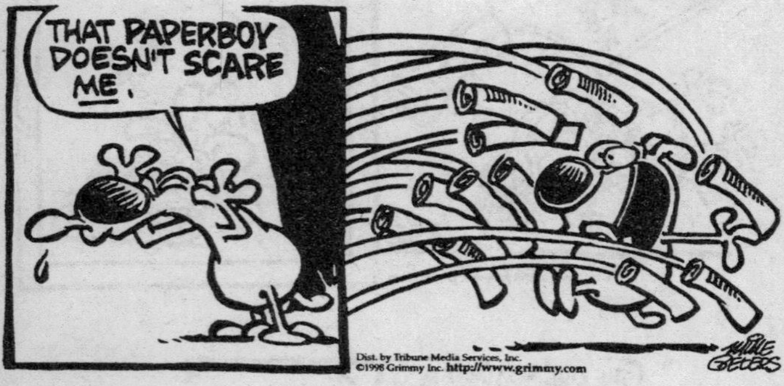
THAT PAPERBOY DOESN'T SCARE ME.
Dist. by Tribune Media Services, Inc.
©1998 Grimmy Inc. http://www.grimmy.com

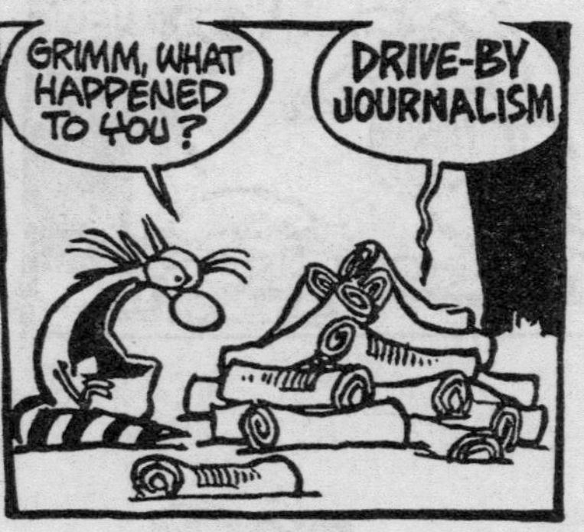
GRIMM, WHAT HAPPENED TO YOU?
DRIVE-BY JOURNALISM

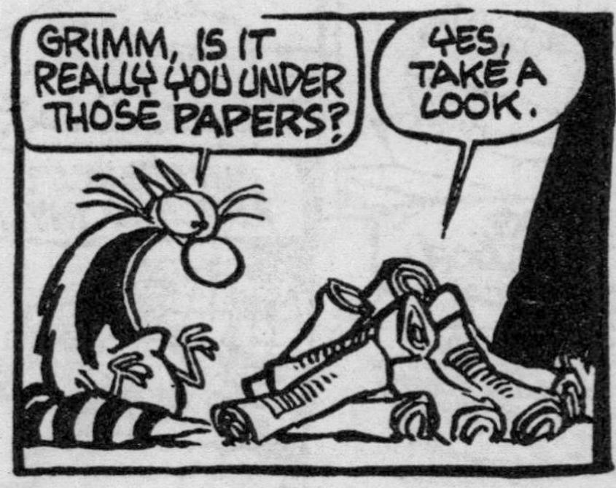
GRIMM, IS IT REALLY YOU UNDER THOSE PAPERS?
YES, TAKE A LOOK.

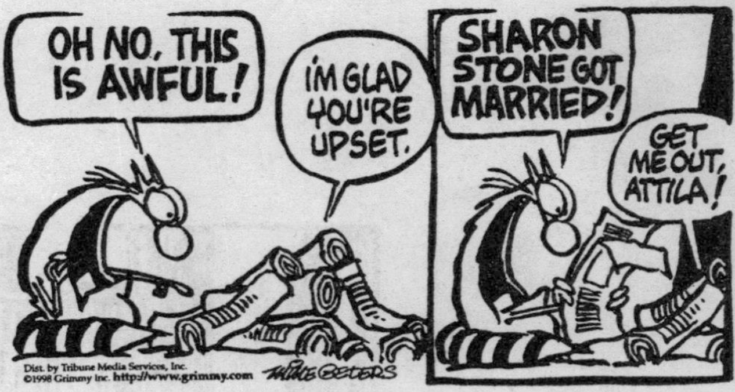
OH NO. THIS IS AWFUL!
I'M GLAD YOU'RE UPSET.
SHARON STONE GOT MARRIED!
GET ME OUT, ATTILA!
Dist. by Tribune Media Services, Inc.
©1998 Grimmy Inc. http://www.grimmy.com

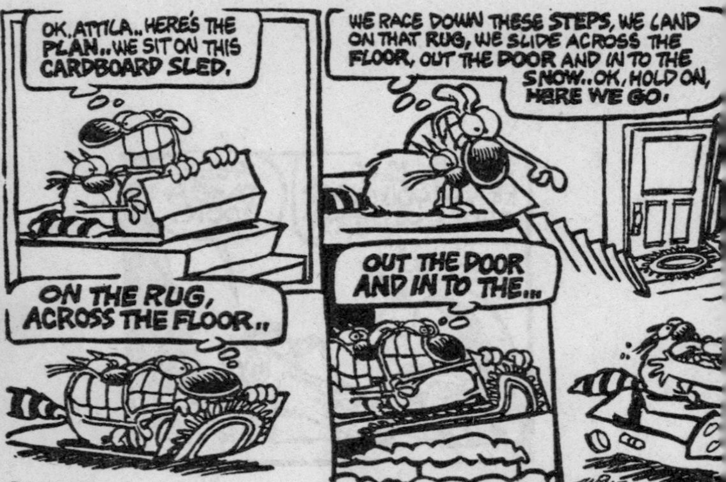
OK, ATTILA.. HERE'S THE PLAN.. WE SIT ON THIS CARDBOARD SLED.
WE RACE DOWN THESE STEPS, WE LAND ON THAT RUG, WE SLIDE ACROSS THE FLOOR, OUT THE DOOR AND IN TO THE SNOW..OK, HOLD ON, HERE WE GO.
ON THE RUG, ACROSS THE FLOOR..
OUT THE DOOR AND IN TO THE...

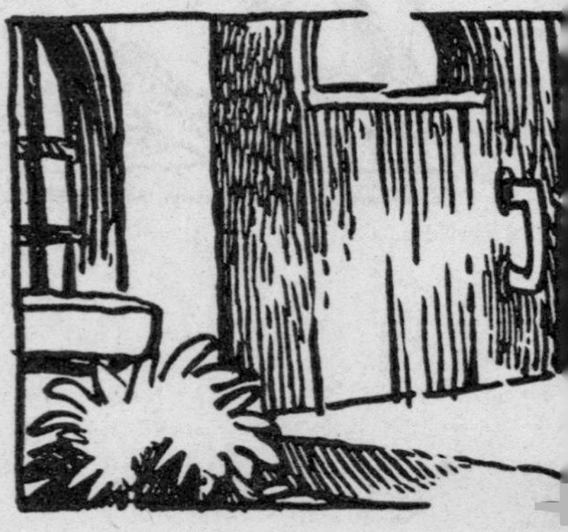

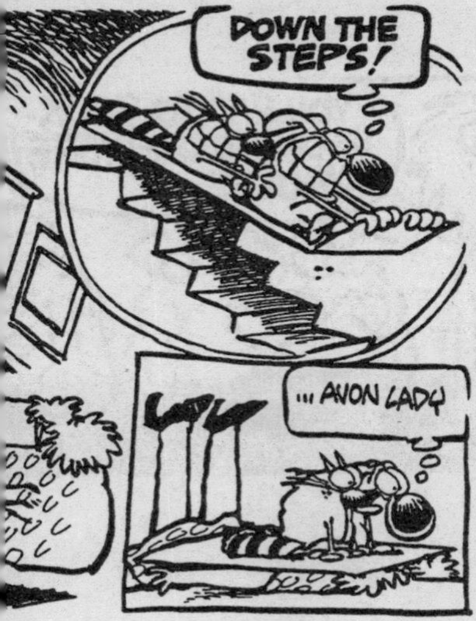
DOWN THE STEPS!
... AVON LADY

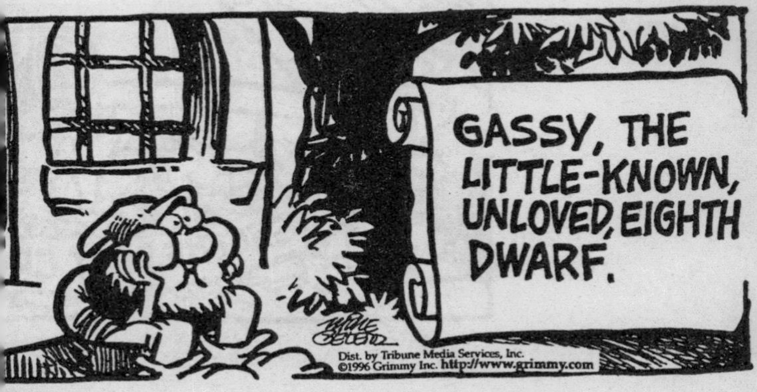
GASSY, THE LITTLE-KNOWN, UNLOVED, EIGHTH DWARF.
Dist. by Tribune Media Services, Inc.
©1996 Grimmy Inc. http://www.grimmy.com

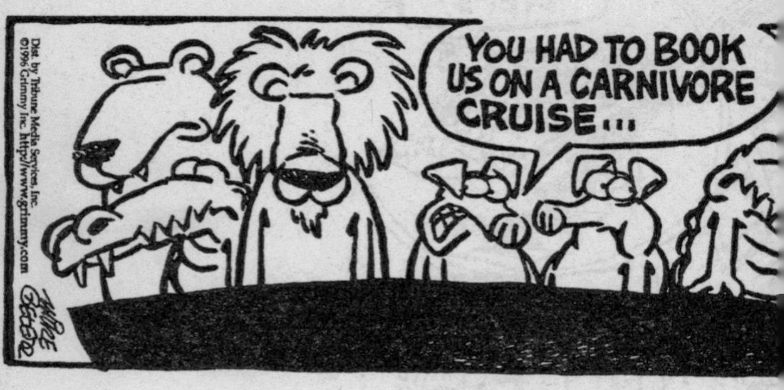
YOU HAD TO BOOK US ON A CARNIVORE CRUISE...
Dist. by Tribune Media Services, Inc. ©1996 Grimmy Inc. http://www.grimmy.com

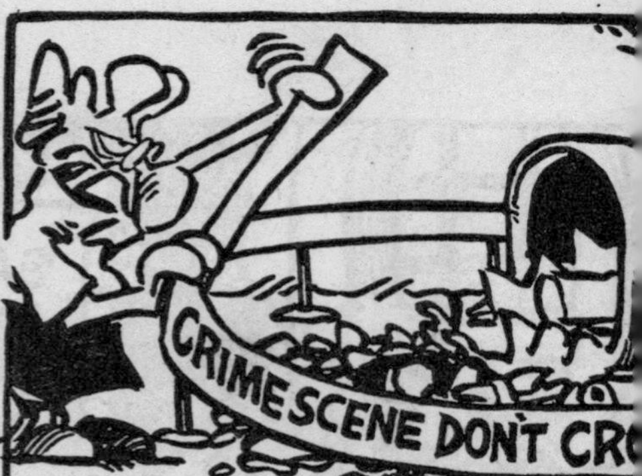
CRIME SCENE DON'T CR

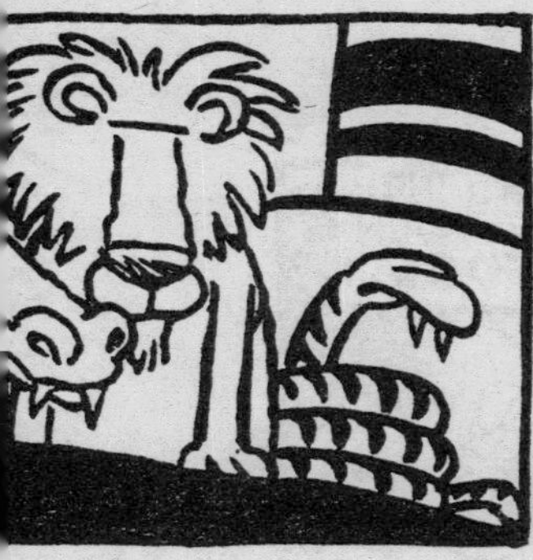

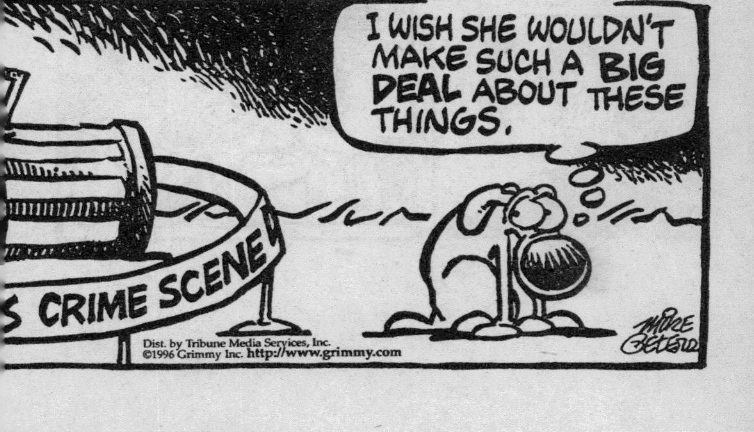
I WISH SHE WOULDN'T MAKE SUCH A BIG DEAL ABOUT THESE THINGS.
S CRIME SCENE
Dist. by Tribune Media Services, Inc.
©1996 Grimmy Inc. http://www.grimmy.com

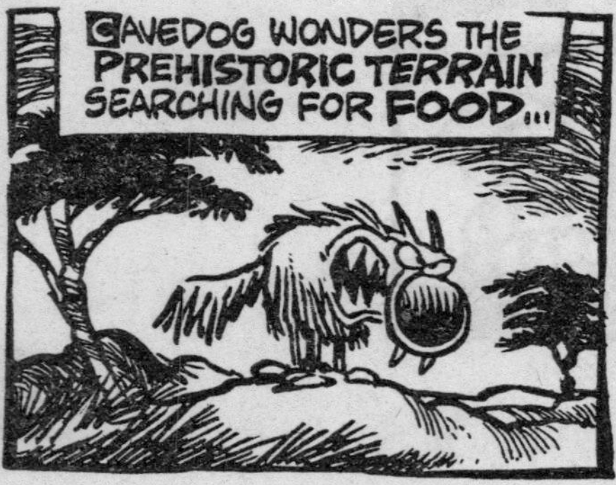
CAVEDOG WONDERS THE PREHISTORIC TERRAIN SEARCHING FOR FOOD...

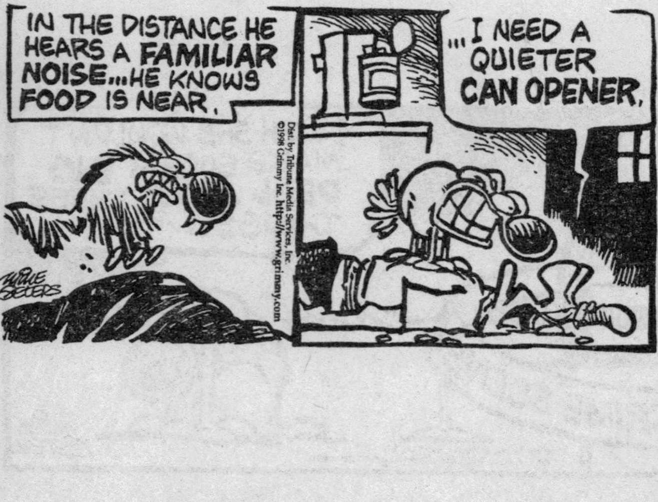
IN THE DISTANCE HE HEARS A FAMILIAR NOISE...HE KNOWS FOOD IS NEAR.
...I NEED A QUIETER CAN OPENER.
Dist. by Tribune Media Services, Inc.
©1998 Grimmy Inc. http://www.grimmy.com
MIKE PETERS

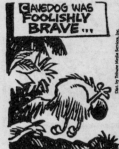

CAVEDOG WAS FOOLISHLY BRAVE...
Dist. by Tribune Media Services, Inc. ©1998 Grimmy Inc. http://www.grimmy.com
HE WOULD SOMETIMES LEAP OUT OF THE FOREST AND CHARGE A DINOSAUR.
DID YOU JUST HEAR A BUMP?

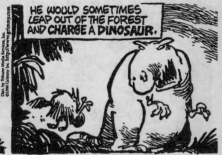

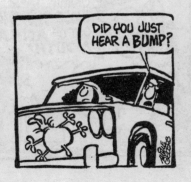

CAVEDOG IS ALWAYS ON THE LOOKOUT FOR HIS ENEMY, THE SABRE-TOOTHED TIGER...
THIS CAT'S LONG SHARP TEETH COULD TEAR RIGHT THROUGH CAVEDOG.
MIKE PETERS
Dist. by Tribune Media Services, Inc.
©1998 Grimmy Inc. http://www.grimmy.com

GRIMM, TAKE THOSE CHOPSTICKS OUT OF ATTILA'S MOUTH!

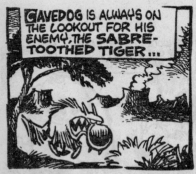

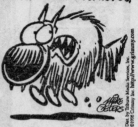

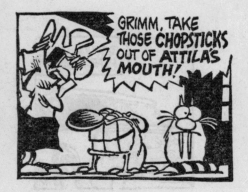

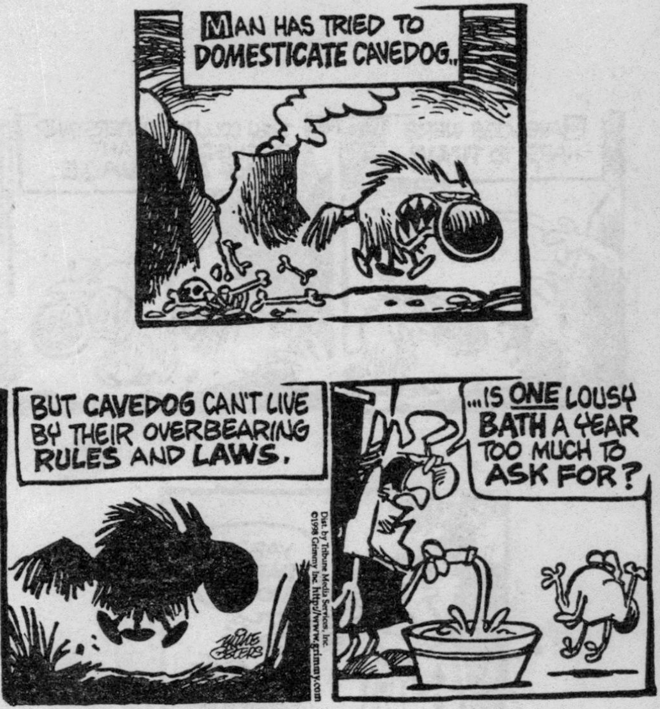
MAN HAS TRIED TO DOMESTICATE CAVEDOG..
BUT CAVEDOG CAN'T LIVE BY THEIR OVERBEARING RULES AND LAWS.
...IS ONE LOUSY BATH A YEAR TOO MUCH TO ASK FOR?
Dist. by Tribune Media Services, Inc.
©1998 Grimmy Inc. http://www.grimmy.com

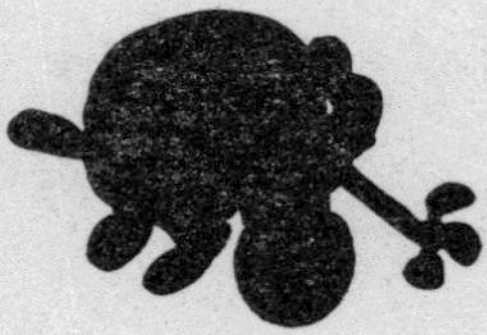

CAVEDOGS WERE HARD TO TRAIN...
THEY COULDN'T UNDERSTAND PREHISTORIC MAN'S EARLY LANGUAGE.
Dist. by Tribune Media Services, Inc.
©1998 Grimmy Inc. http://www.grimmy.com
YABBA DABBA DOO?

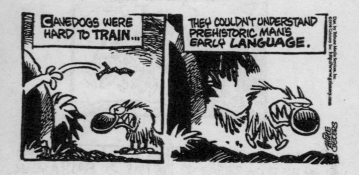

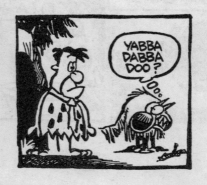

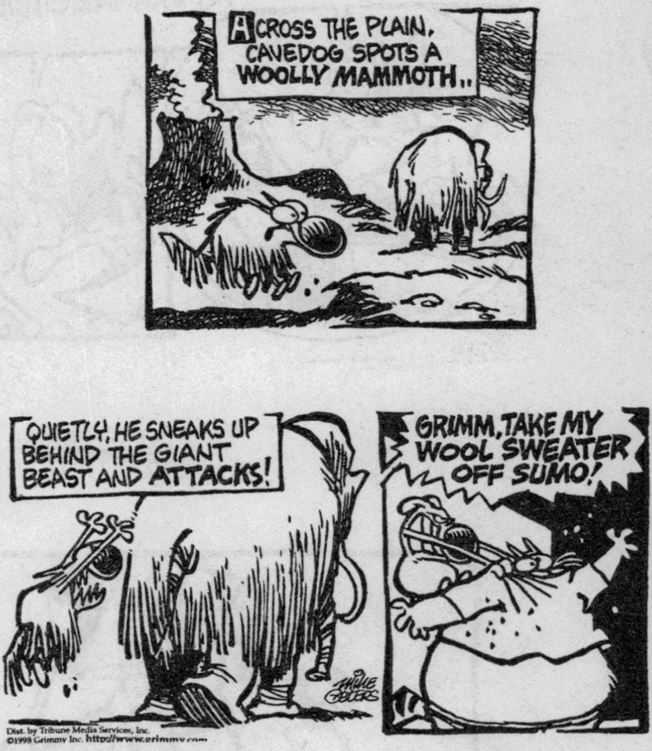
ACROSS THE PLAIN, CAVEDOG SPOTS A WOOLLY MAMMOTH..
QUIETLY, HE SNEAKS UP BEHIND THE GIANT BEAST AND ATTACKS!
GRIMM, TAKE MY WOOL SWEATER OFF SUMO!

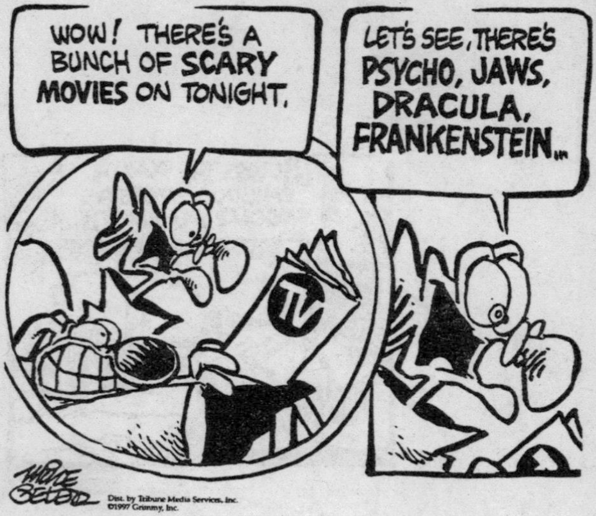
WOW! THERE'S A BUNCH OF SCARY MOVIES ON TONIGHT.
LET'S SEE, THERE'S PSYCHO, JAWS, DRACULA, FRANKENSTEIN...

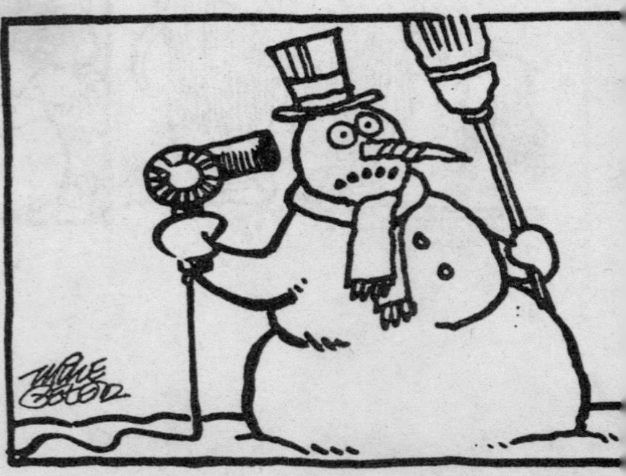

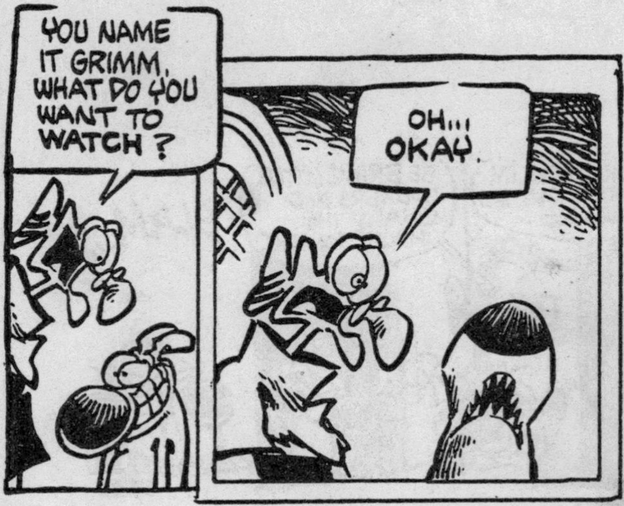
YOU NAME IT GRIMM, WHAT DO YOU WANT TO WATCH?
OH... OKAY.

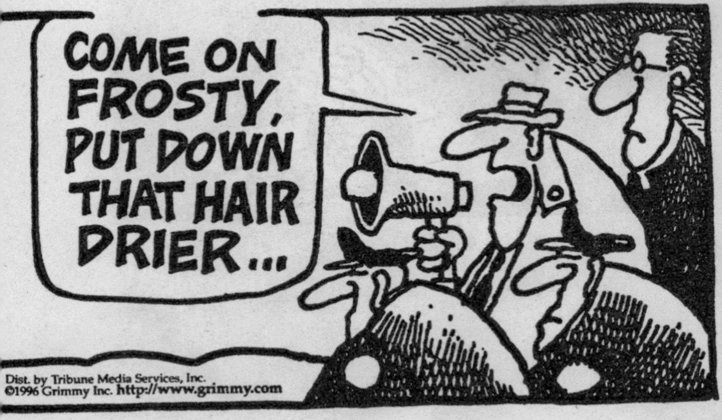
COME ON FROSTY, PUT DOWN THAT HAIR DRIER...

OKAY BOYS, I'M GOING OUT THIS EVENING...
BE BRAVE LITTLE SOLDIERS AND GUARD THE HOUSE TONIGHT.
SLAM...

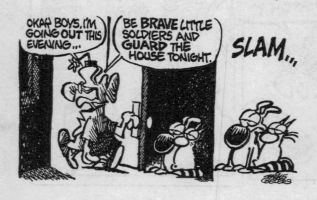

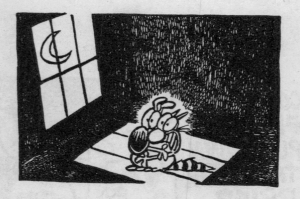

SHE WANTS US
TO GUARD THE
HOUSE FROM
BURGLARS

I DON'T SEE ANY
BURGLARS
UNDER THIS
BED.
GOOD...
OUR JOB
IS DONE!
ZIP...

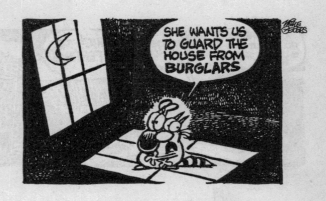

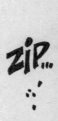

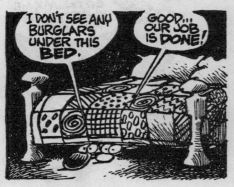

YOU'RE THE DOG, YOU GO OUT AND GUARD THE HOUSE.
I'M NOT A GUARD DOG, I'M A WATCH DOG.
WHAT'S THE DIFFERENCE?
Dist. by Tribune Media Services, Inc. ©1998 Grimmy, Inc. http://www.grimmy.com
GO ON..ASK ME WHAT TIME IT IS...

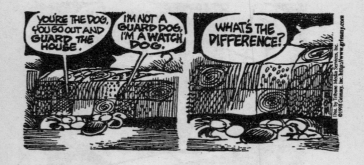

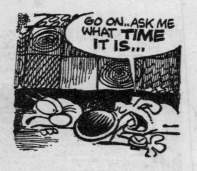

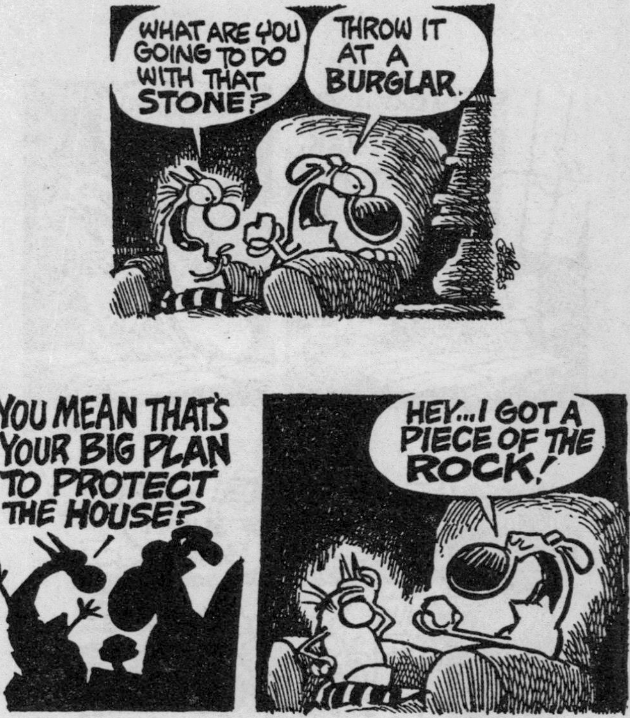
WHAT ARE YOU GOING TO DO WITH THAT STONE?
THROW IT AT A BURGLAR.
YOU MEAN THAT'S YOUR BIG PLAN TO PROTECT THE HOUSE?
HEY...I GOT A PIECE OF THE ROCK!

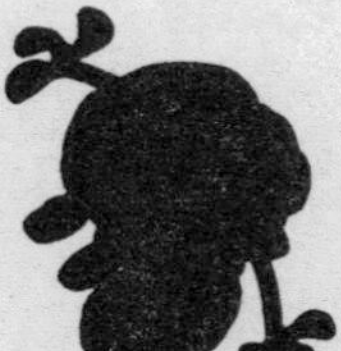

I'M COLD, HUNGRY AND I'M AFRAID OF THE DARK.
OKAY, OKAY, COME WITH ME.

.. NOW I'M JUST COLD.
HEY, 2 OUT OF 3 ISN'T BAD.
MILK

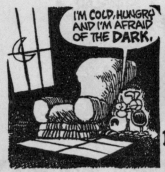

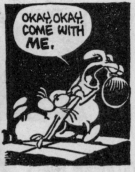

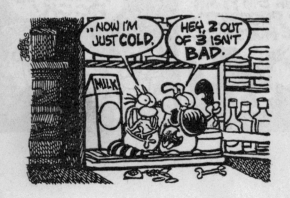

IT'S SO DARK IN HERE. TURN ON THE LIGHT SWITCH.
I'M TRYING TO BUT I DON'T HAVE THE RIGHT EQUIPMENT.
WHAT KIND OF EQUIPMENT?
...A THUMB!

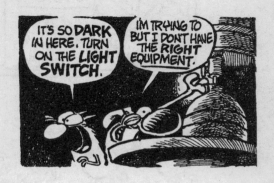

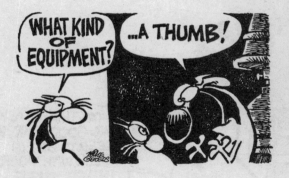

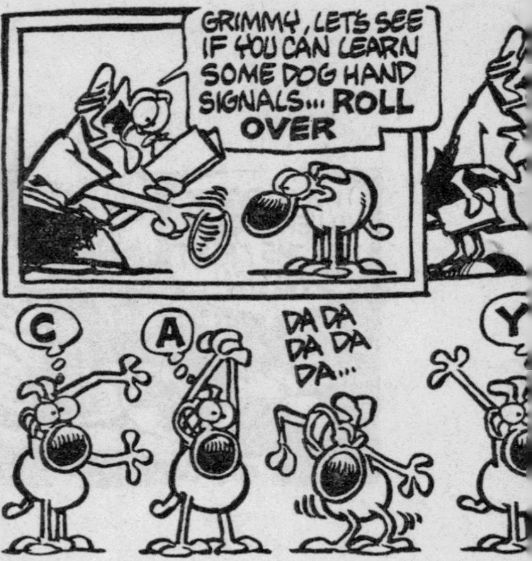
GRIMMY, LET'S SEE IF YOU CAN LEARN SOME DOG HAND SIGNALS... ROLL OVER
C
A
DA DA DA DA DA...
Y

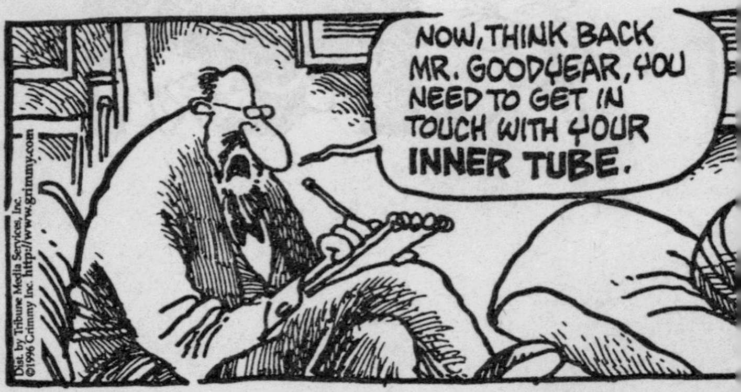
NOW, THINK BACK MR. GOODYEAR, YOU NEED TO GET IN TOUCH WITH YOUR INNER TUBE.
Dist. by Tribune Media Services, Inc.
©1996 Grimmy Inc. http://www.grimmy.com

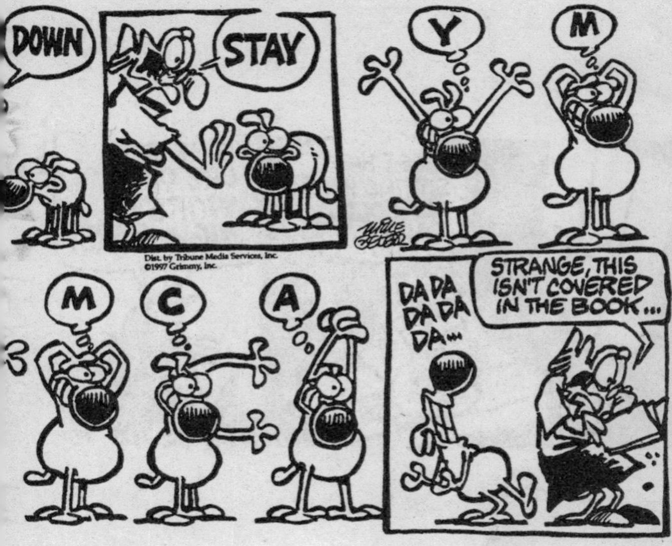
DOWN
STAY
Dist. by Tribune Media Services, Inc.
©1997 Grimmy, Inc.
Y
M
M
C
A
DA DA DA DA DA...
STRANGE, THIS ISN'T COVERED IN THE BOOK...

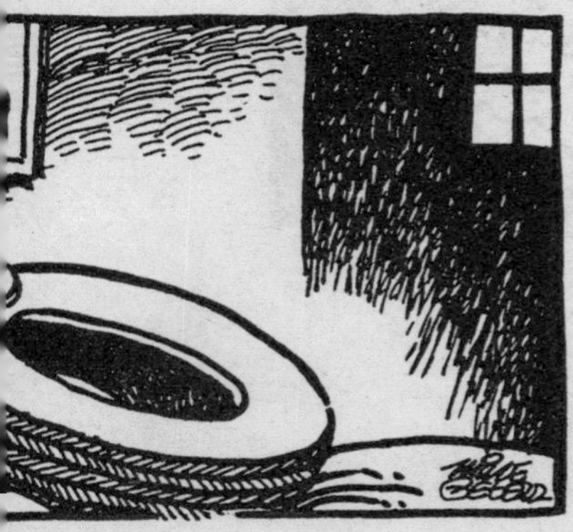

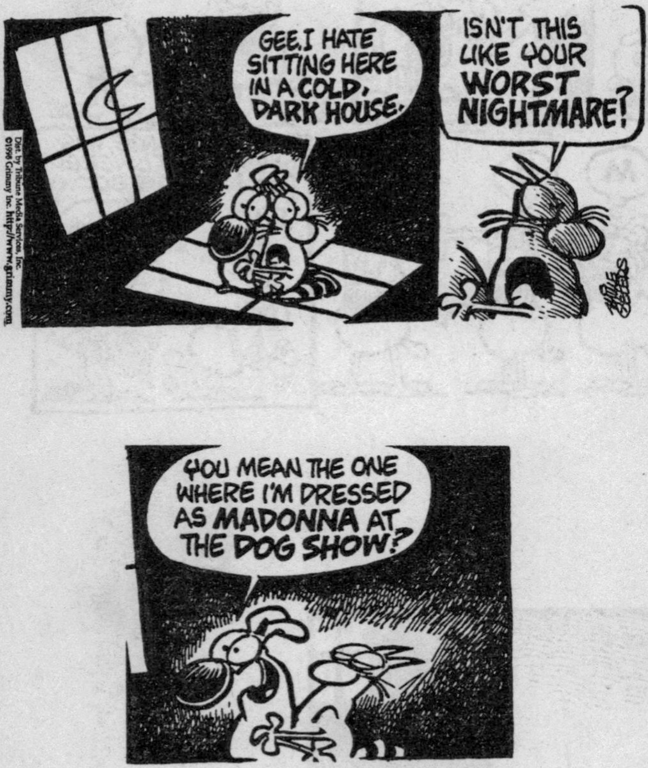
GEE, I HATE SITTING HERE IN A COLD, DARK HOUSE.
ISN'T THIS LIKE YOUR WORST NIGHTMARE?
YOU MEAN THE ONE WHERE I'M DRESSED AS MADONNA AT THE DOG SHOW?
Dist. by Tribune Media Services, Inc. ©1996 Grimmy Inc. http://www.grimmy.com

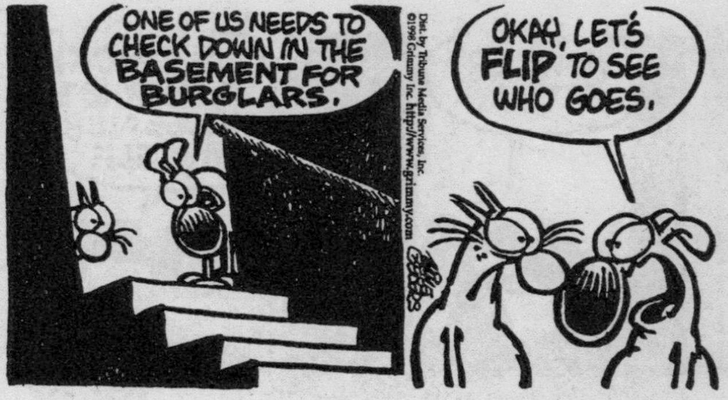
ONE OF US NEEDS TO CHECK DOWN IN THE BASEMENT FOR BURGLARS.
Dist. by Tribune Media Services, Inc. ©1998 Grimmy Inc. http://www.grimmy.com
OKAY, LET'S FLIP TO SEE WHO GOES.

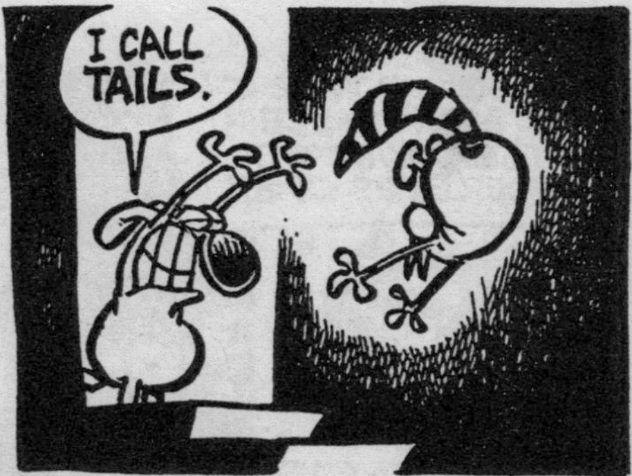
I CALL TAILS.

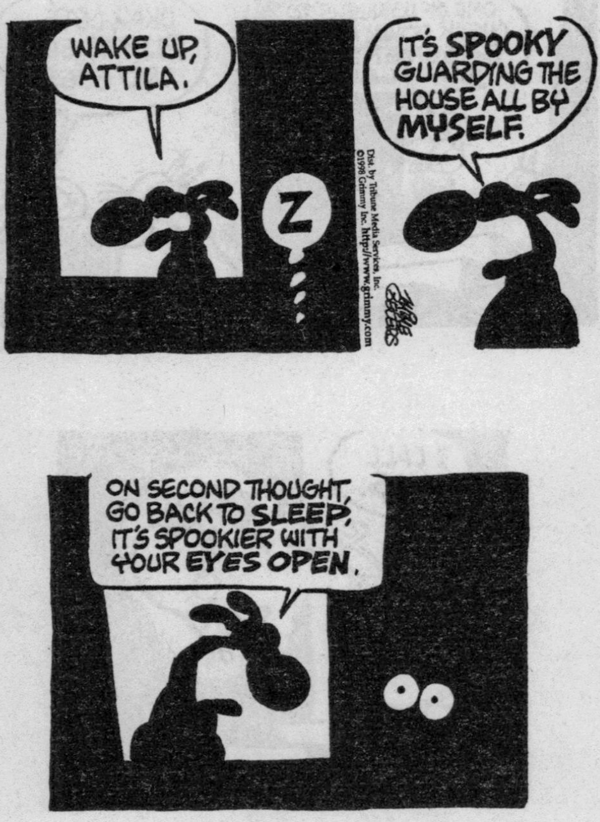
WAKE UP, ATTILA.
Z
Dist. by Tribune Media Services, Inc.
©1998 Grimmy Inc. http://www.grimmy.com
IT'S SPOOKY GUARDING THE HOUSE ALL BY MYSELF.
ON SECOND THOUGHT, GO BACK TO SLEEP, IT'S SPOOKIER WITH YOUR EYES OPEN.

WE CAN'T FIGHT OFF A BURGLAR, NEITHER ONE OF US IS A GUARD DOG.
Dist. by Tribune Media Services, Inc. ©1998 Grimmy Inc. http://www.grimmy.com
I WISH WE KNEW KARATE.
WHY..? IS HE A GUARD DOG?

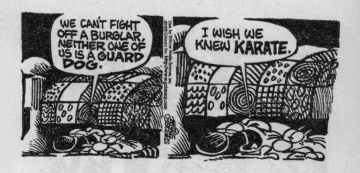

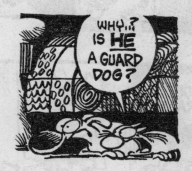

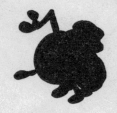

ARE YOU SURE WE'RE SAFE IN HERE?
DON'T WORRY, NOBODY CAN SNEAK IN...I COVERED THE LIVING ROOM FLOOR WITH...
SNAP
...MOUSE TRAPS.
MIKE PETERS
Dist. by Tribune Media Services, Inc. ©1998 Grimmy Inc. http://www.grimmy.com

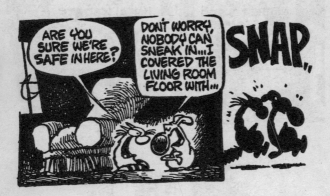

IT'S NICE HAVING HER BACK HOME...
ALTHOUGH, I WASN'T SCARED AT ALL.
ME NEITHER
Dist. by Tribune Media Services, Inc.
©1998 Grimmy Inc. http://www.grimmy.com
Z

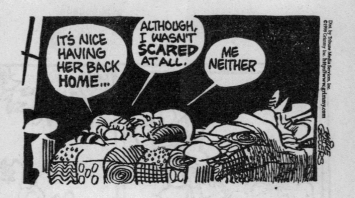

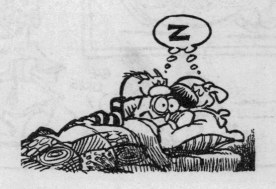

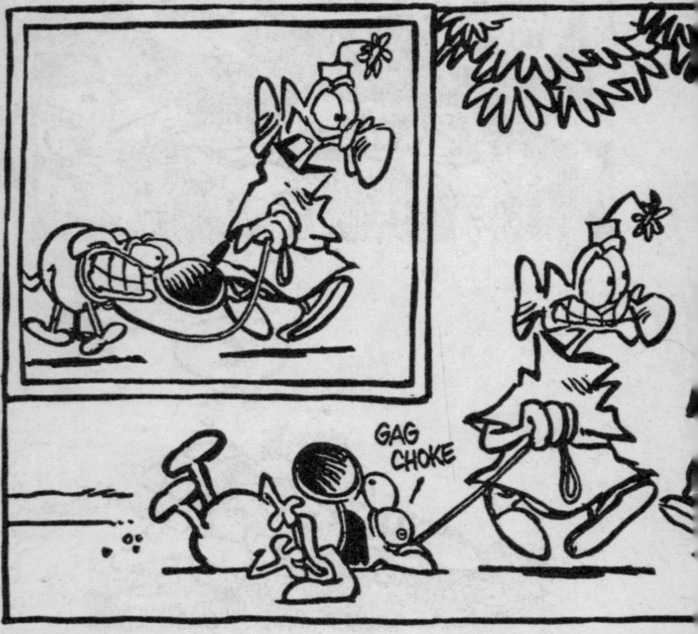
GAG
CHOKE
!

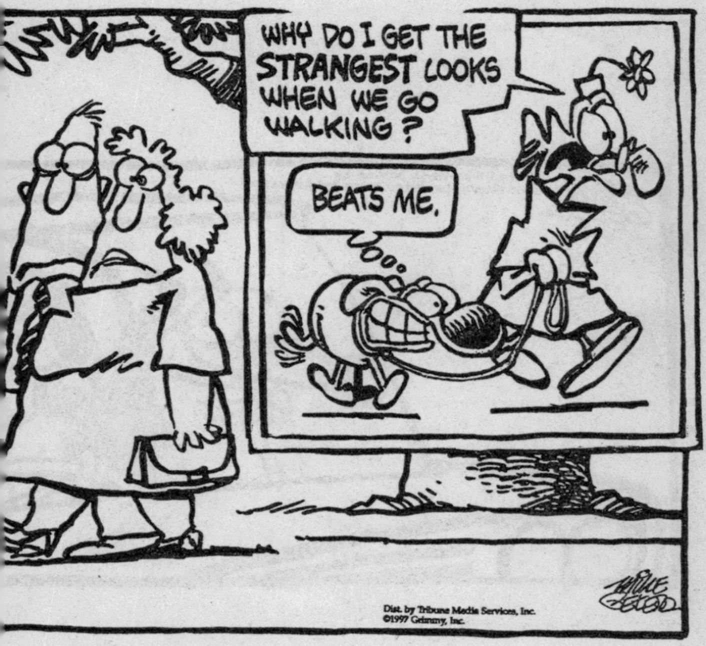
WHY DO I GET THE STRANGEST LOOKS WHEN WE GO WALKING?
BEATS ME.
Dist. by Tribune Media Services, Inc.
©1997 Grimmy, Inc.

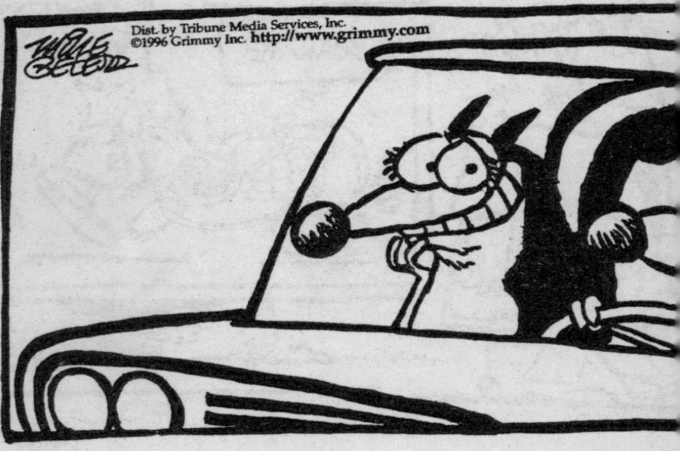
Dist. by Tribune Media Services, Inc.
©1996 Grimmy Inc. http://www.grimmy.com

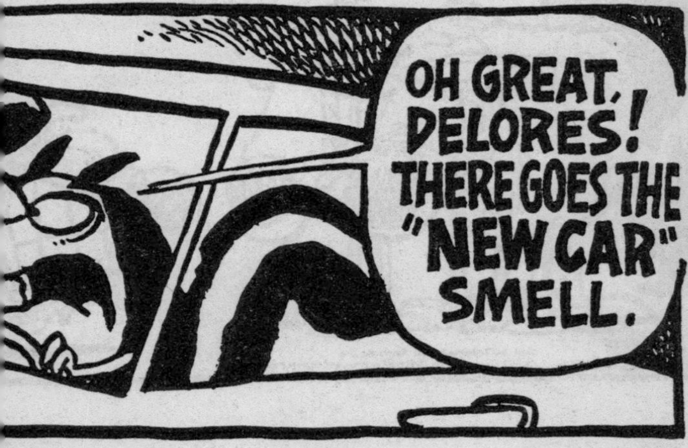
OH GREAT, DELORES! THERE GOES THE "NEW CAR" SMELL.

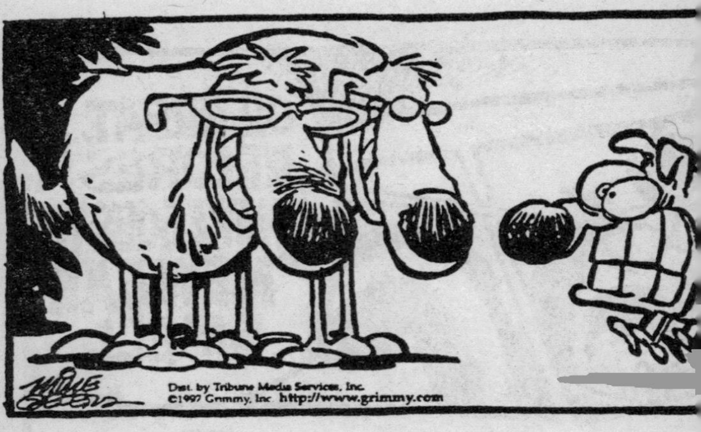
Dist. by Tribune Media Services, Inc.
©1997 Grimmy, Inc. http://www.grimmy.com

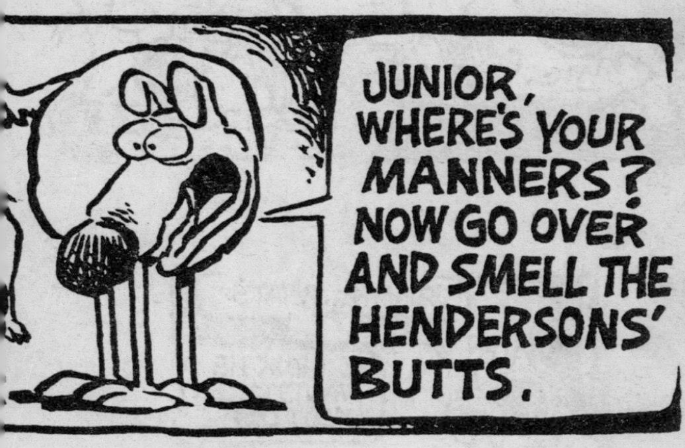
JUNIOR, WHERE'S YOUR MANNERS? NOW GO OVER AND SMELL THE HENDERSONS' BUTTS.

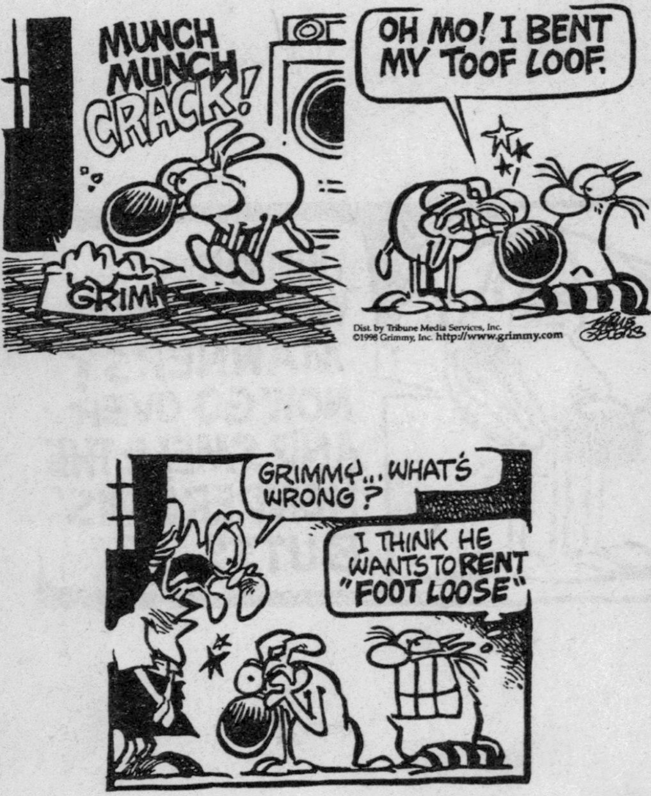
MUNCH
MUNCH
CRACK!
GRIM
OH MO! I BENT MY TOOF LOOF.
Dist. by Tribune Media Services, Inc.
©1998 Grimmy, Inc. http://www.grimmy.com
GRIMMY... WHAT'S WRONG?
I THINK HE WANTS TO RENT "FOOT LOOSE"

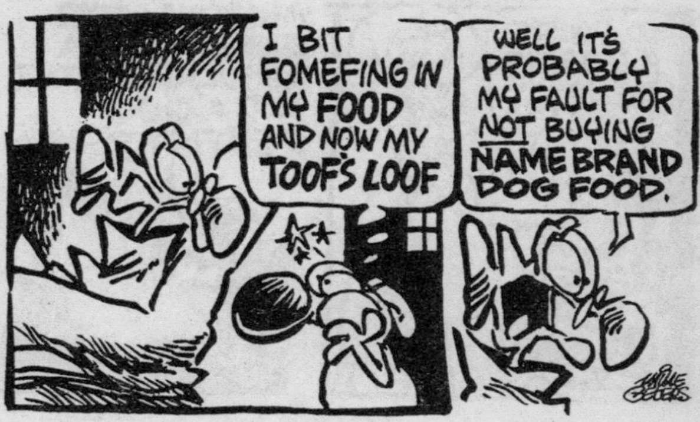
I BIT FOMEFING IN MY FOOD AND NOW MY TOOF'S LOOF
WELL IT'S PROBABLY MY FAULT FOR NOT BUYING NAME BRAND DOG FOOD.

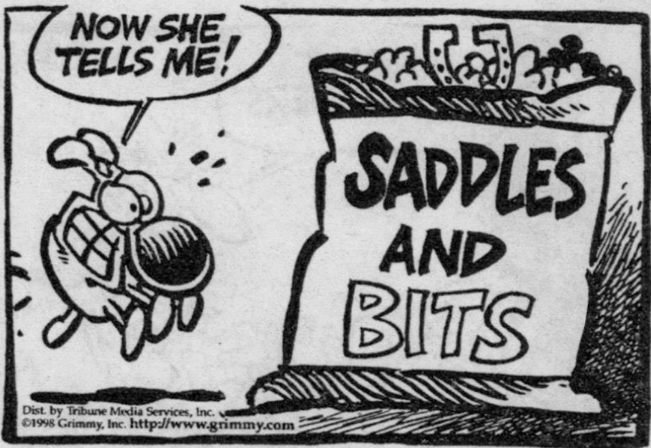
NOW SHE TELLS ME!
SADDLES AND BITS
Dist. by Tribune Media Services, Inc.
©1998 Grimmy, Inc. http://www.grimmy.com

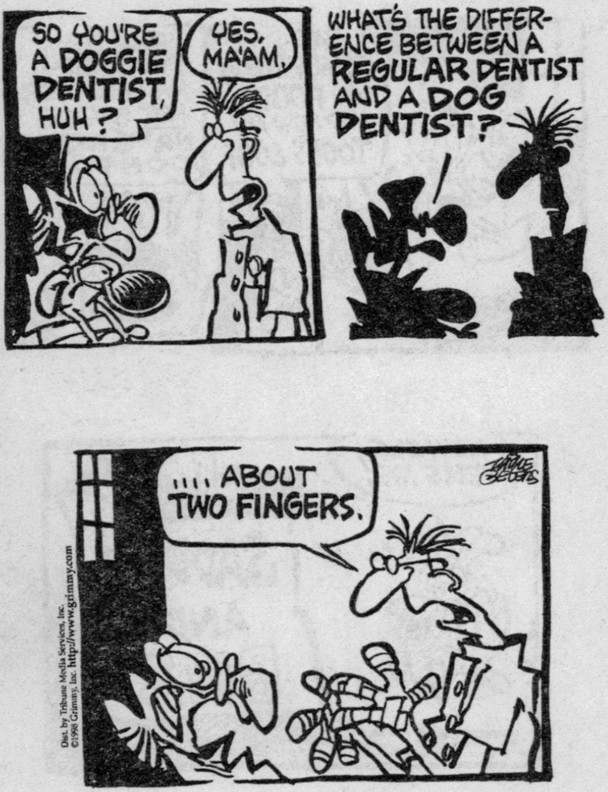
SO YOU'RE A DOGGIE DENTIST, HUH ?
YES, MA'AM.
WHAT'S THE DIFFERENCE BETWEEN A REGULAR DENTIST AND A DOG DENTIST ?
.... ABOUT TWO FINGERS.
Mike Peters

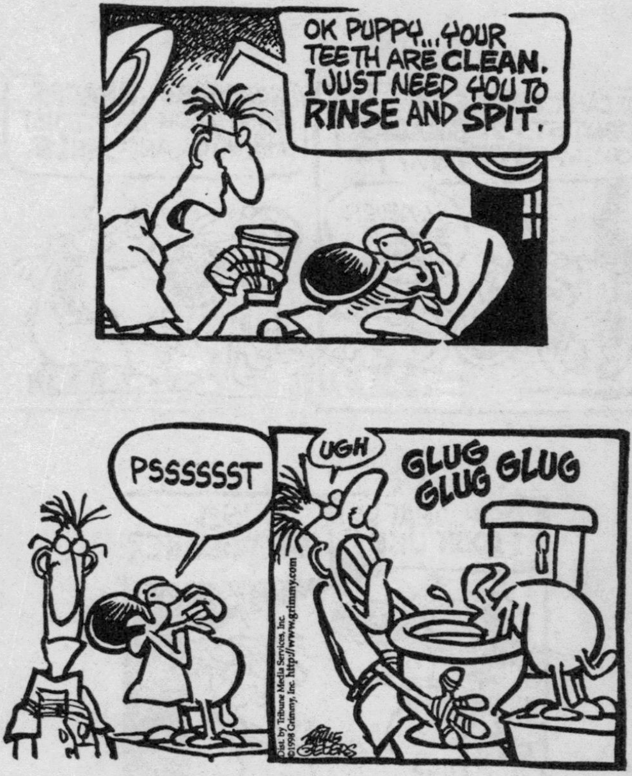
OK PUPPY... YOUR TEETH ARE CLEAN. I JUST NEED YOU TO RINSE AND SPIT.
PSSSSSST
UGH
GLUG GLUG GLUG
Dist. by Tribune Media Services, Inc.
©1998 Grimmy, Inc. http://www.grimmy.com

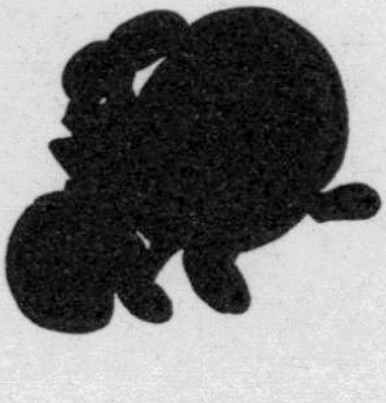

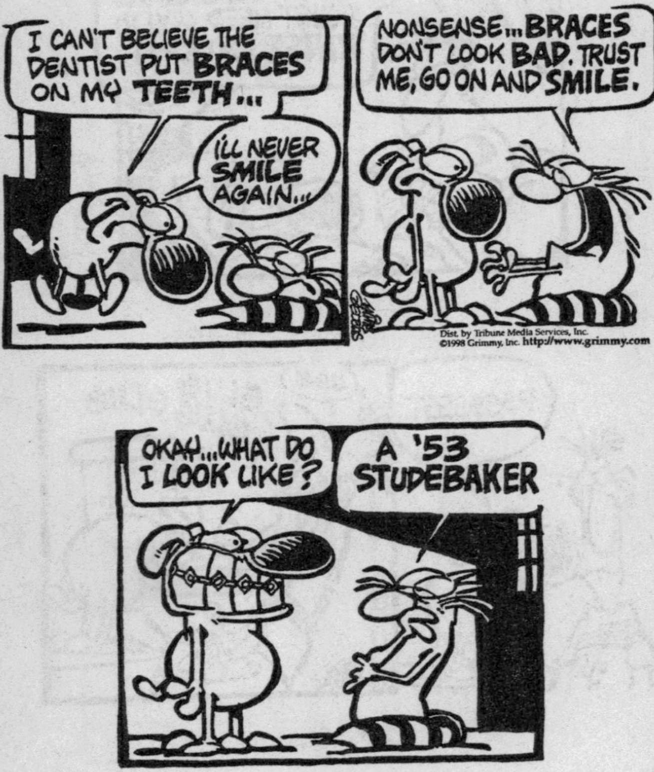
I CAN'T BELIEVE THE DENTIST PUT BRACES ON MY TEETH...
I'LL NEVER SMILE AGAIN...
NONSENSE... BRACES DON'T LOOK BAD. TRUST ME, GO ON AND SMILE.
OKAY... WHAT DO I LOOK LIKE?
A '53 STUDEBAKER

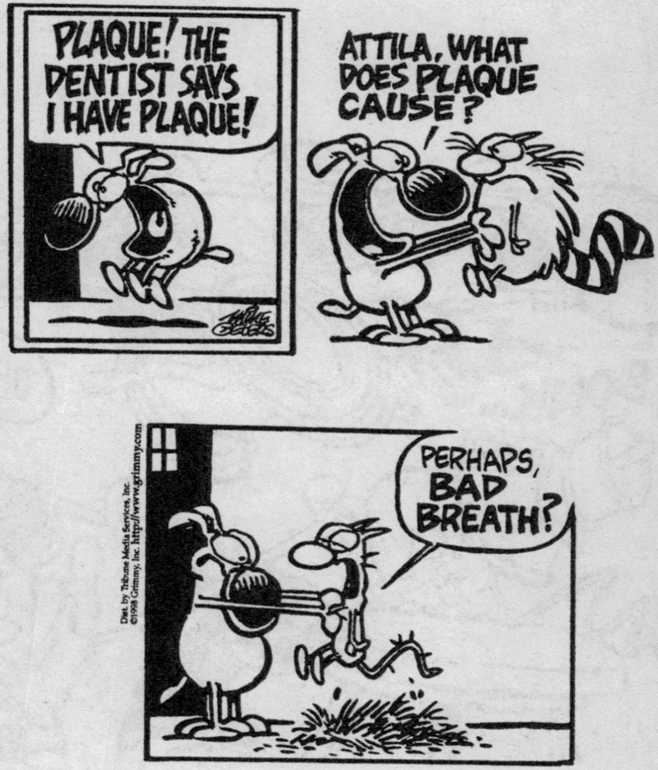
PLAQUE! THE DENTIST SAYS I HAVE PLAQUE!
ATTILA, WHAT DOES PLAQUE CAUSE?
PERHAPS, BAD BREATH?

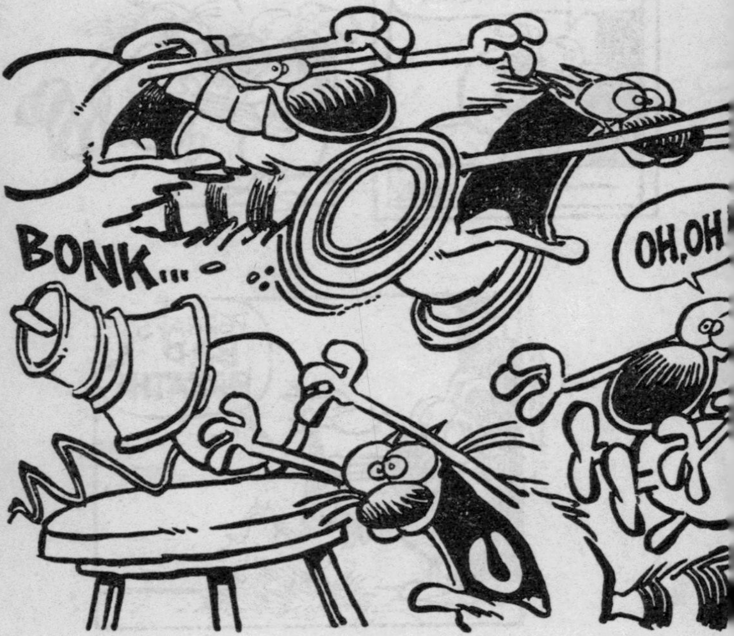
BONK...
OH,OH

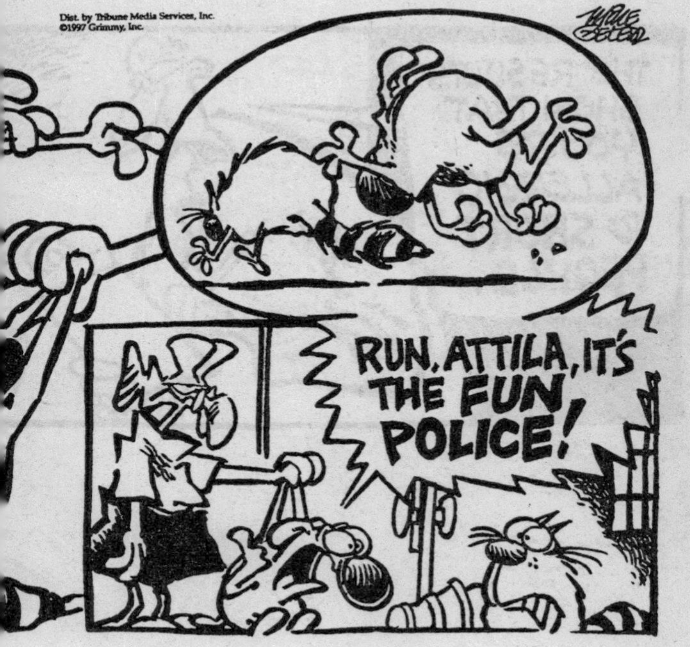
Dist. by Tribune Media Services, Inc.
©1997 Grimmy, Inc.
RUN, ATTILA, IT'S THE FUN POLICE!

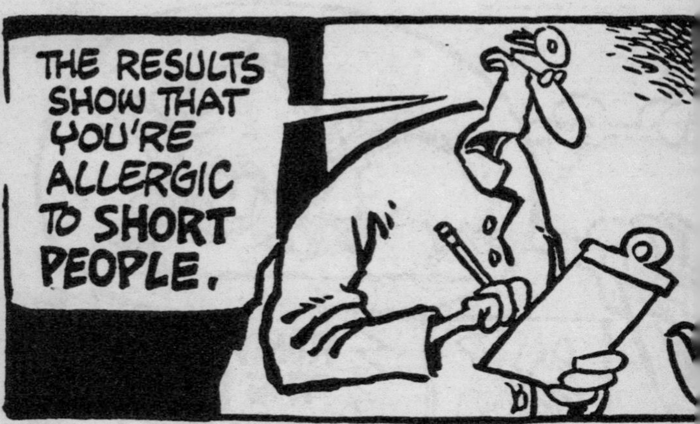
THE RESULTS SHOW THAT YOU'RE ALLERGIC TO SHORT PEOPLE.

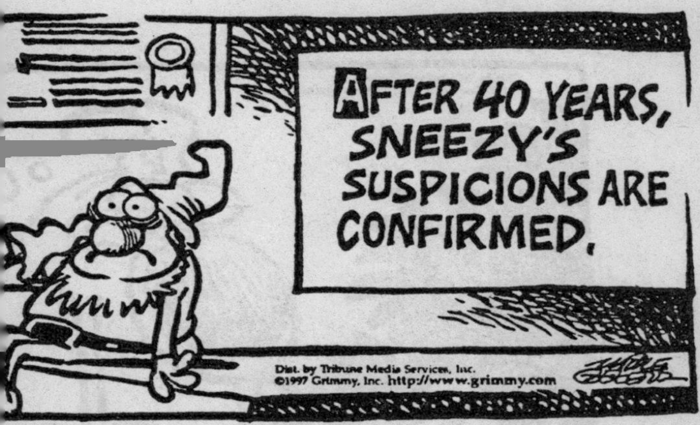
AFTER 40 YEARS, SNEEZY'S SUSPICIONS ARE CONFIRMED.
Dist. by Tribune Media Services, Inc.
©1997 Grimmy, Inc. http://www.grimmy.com

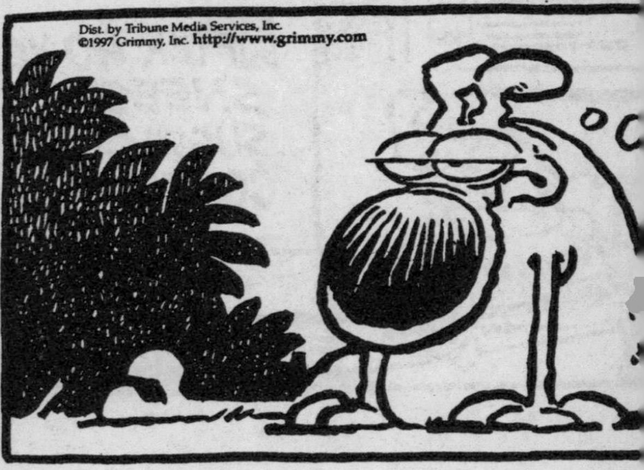
Dist. by Tribune Media Services, Inc.
©1997 Grimmy, Inc. http://www.grimmy.com

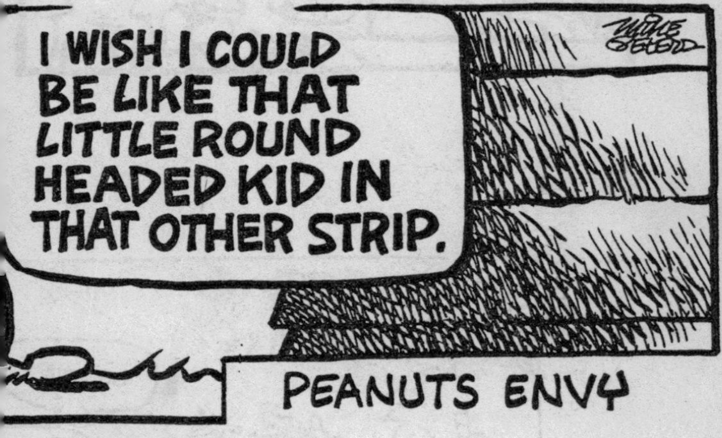
I WISH I COULD BE LIKE THAT LITTLE ROUND HEADED KID IN THAT OTHER STRIP.

PEANUTS ENVY

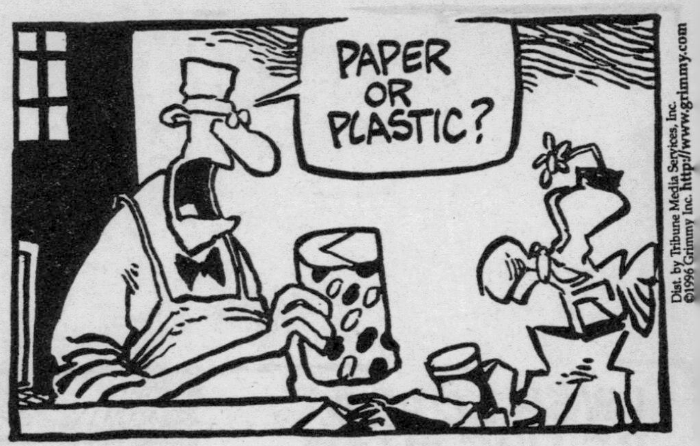
PAPER OR PLASTIC?
Dist. by Tribune Media Services, Inc.
©1996 Grimmy Inc. http://www.grimmy.com

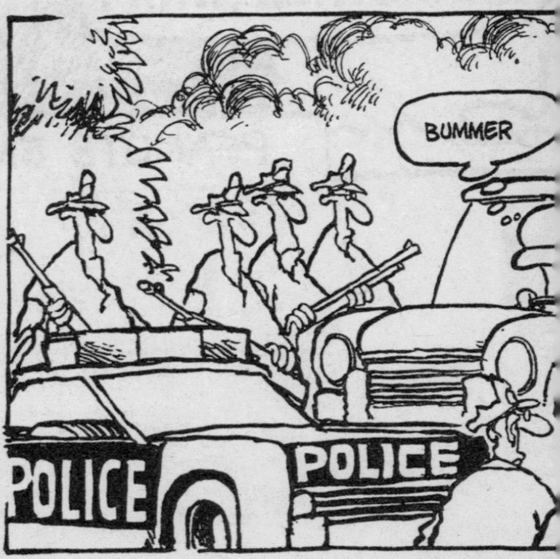
BUMMER
POLICE
POLICE

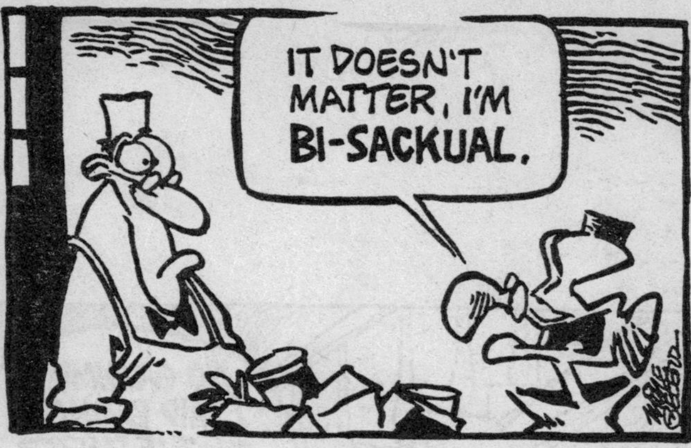
IT DOESN'T MATTER, I'M BI-SACKUAL.

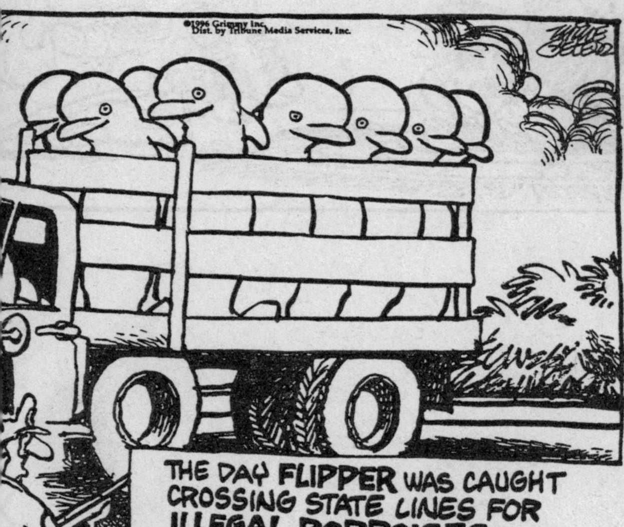
©1996 Grimmy Inc.
Dist. by Tribune Media Services, Inc.

THE DAY **FLIPPER** WAS CAUGHT CROSSING STATE LINES FOR **ILLEGAL PORPOISES.**

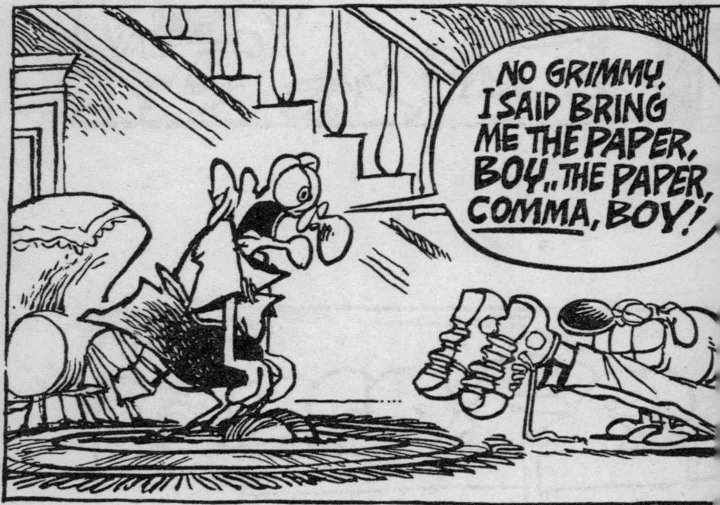
NO GRIMMY, I SAID BRING ME THE PAPER, BOY.. THE PAPER, COMMA, BOY!

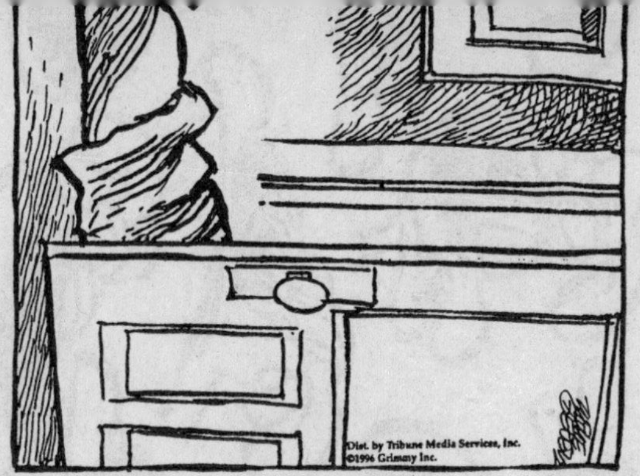
Dist. by Tribune Media Services, Inc.
©1996 Grimmy Inc.

Dist. by Tribune Media Services, Inc.
©1996 Grimmy Inc.

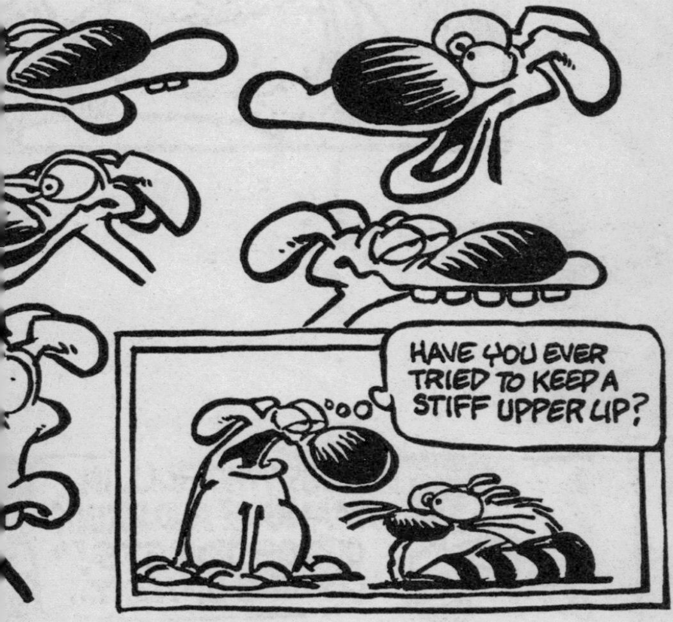
HAVE YOU EVER TRIED TO KEEP A STIFF UPPER LIP?

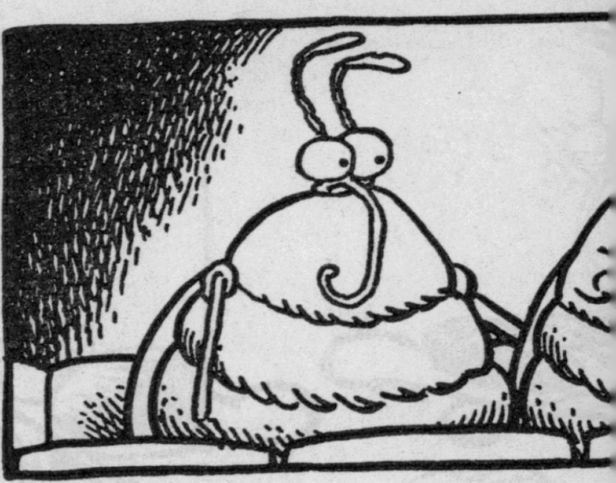

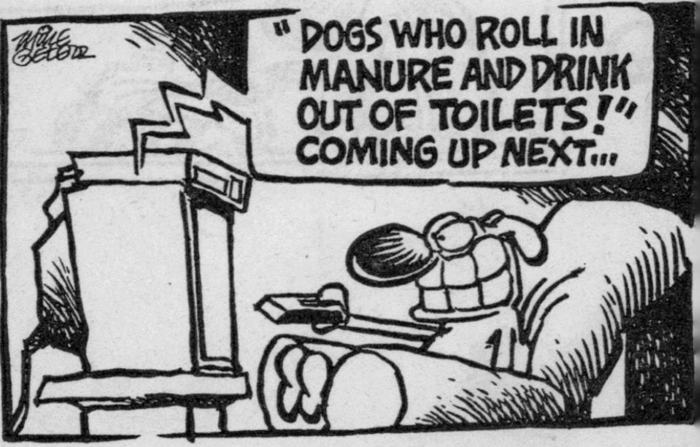
"DOGS WHO ROLL IN MANURE AND DRINK OUT OF TOILETS!" COMING UP NEXT...

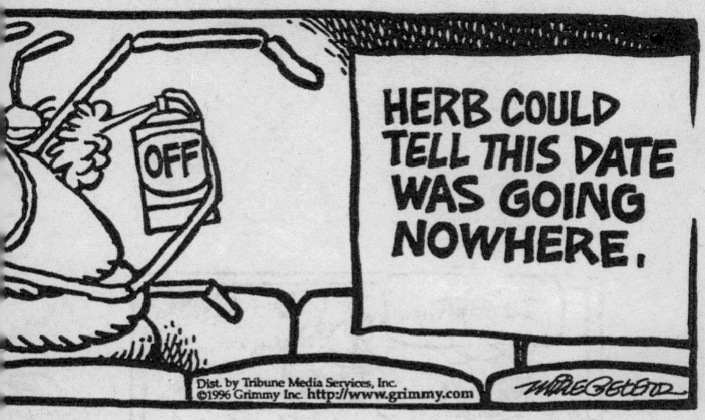
OFF
HERB COULD TELL THIS DATE WAS GOING NOWHERE.
Dist. by Tribune Media Services, Inc.
©1996 Grimmy Inc. http://www.grimmy.com

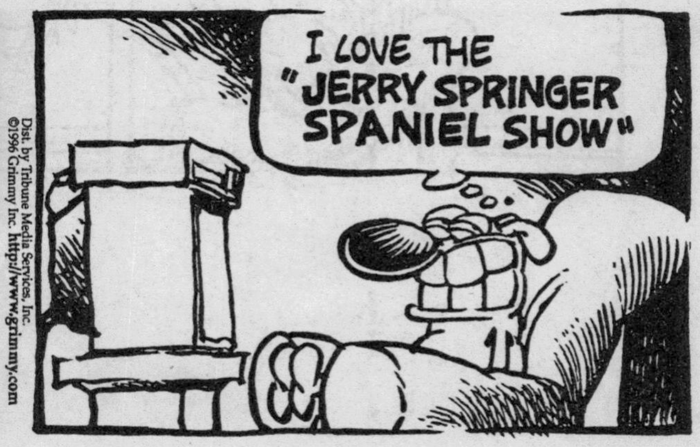
I LOVE THE "JERRY SPRINGER SPANIEL SHOW"
Dist. by Tribune Media Services, Inc.
©1996 Grimmy Inc. http://www.grimmy.com

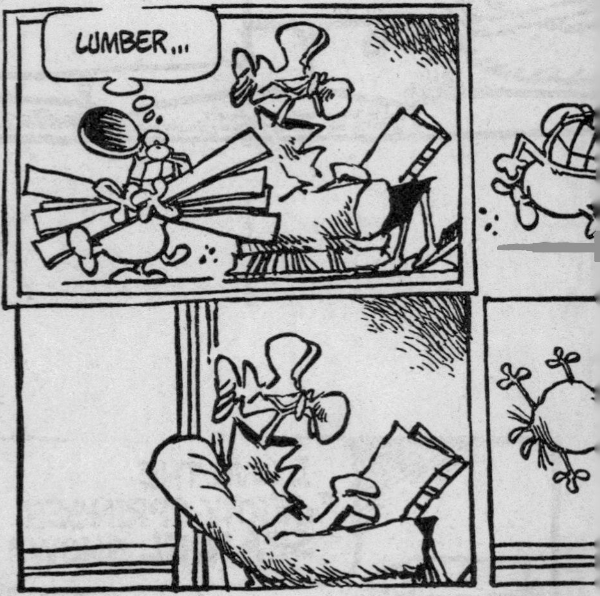
LUMBER...

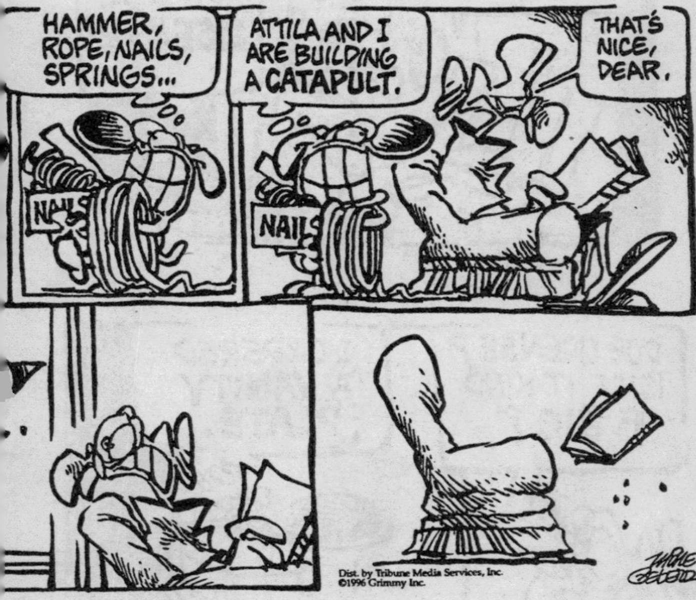
HAMMER, ROPE, NAILS, SPRINGS...
NAILS
ATTILA AND I ARE BUILDING A CATAPULT.
NAILS
THAT'S NICE, DEAR.
Dist. by Tribune Media Services, Inc.
©1996 Grimmy Inc.
MIKE PETERS

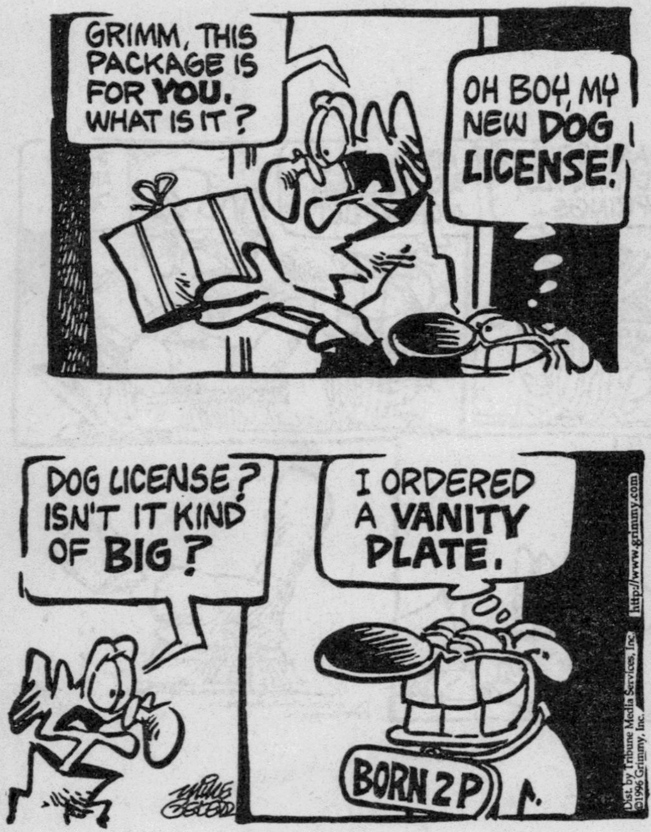
GRIMM, THIS PACKAGE IS FOR **YOU.** WHAT IS IT ?
OH BOY, MY NEW **DOG LICENSE!**
DOG LICENSE? ISN'T IT KIND OF **BIG ?**
I ORDERED A **VANITY PLATE.**
BORN 2 P
Dist. by Tribune Media Services, Inc. ©1996 Grimmy, Inc.
http://www.grimmy.com